English
for
Beginners

اللغة الإنجليزية للمبتدئين

By

Ibrahim A. Abu- Anza

تـأليف

إبراهـيم عبد الرحيم أبوعـنزه

2006

اللغة الإنجليزية للمبتدئين

English for Beginners

الطبعة الأولى ٢٠٠٣

الطبعة الثانية ٢٠٠٦

First Edition 2003

Second Edition 2006

حقوق الطبع محفوظة للمؤلف : إبراهيم عبد الرحيم أبوعنزه .

قطر ــ الدوحة   ص . ب ٣٦٣١٧

هاتف : 59 292 58 / 974+

+974 / 479 00 47

E-mail : abuomar4667@hotmail.com

دار يافا العلمية للطباعة والنشر

عمّان ــ الأردن ــ الأشرفية ص.ب ٥٢٠٦٥١ / تلفاكس   9626+
4778770

رقم الإجازة المتسلسل لدى دائرة المطبوعات والنشر : ١٥٦٦ /٧ / ٢٠٠٣

بـسم الله الـرحـمـن الـرحيـم

قال اللهُ تعـالـى :
" ومـن آيـاتـهِ خـلـقُ الـسـمٰواتِ والأرضِ واخـتـلافُ ألـسنتِكـم وألـوانِكـم . إنَّ في ذلكَ لآياتٍ لـلـعـالـمـيـن . "

Allah (God) says that of His signs are the creation of the heavens and earth as well as the diversity of your languages and colours.

وقـالَ تعـالـى :
" إنَّما يخـشـى اللهَ مـن عـباده العلمـاءُ."

Allah says that of His human creatures the learned ones fear Him.

قال سـيـدنا محمد عـليـه الصلاة والـسـلام :
" مـن تعلَّمَ لغـةَ قومٍ أمِنَ مَكُرهـم. "

The Prophet , Muhammad (pbuh) says that he who learns the language of another community will be safe from their treachery.

Introduction and Dedication

English *for* Beginners is primarily designed for the good of native speakers of Arabic who are willing to learn English. The graded material and the approach allow the learners to proceed smoothly, thus making the learning job accessible.

This book stresses to a great extent the phonetic side of the language departing from the old approach which stresses alphabets at the expense of sounds. Accordingly, the book provides ways to pronounce words correctly moving from the part to the whole and giving sets of words that contain similar phones such as :cast ,fast, last , mast , past and vast.

It is worth saying that sound pronunciation is conducive to the acquisition of a continually growing number of words which is closely linked to the reading skill. This reading skill, if properly developed, can pave the way for the acquisition of other language skills . That is why the book attaches great importance to sound pronunciation as well as the reading skill . It is indisputable that a learner with a sound reading skill can perform well in other language areas.

EFB allows the learner to practise the language by providing model sentence patterns and by presenting the material in a logical way , which makes the language - learning task pleasant and worthwhile.

I have stressed , throughout the book , the integration of all the language skills without doing any injustice to a particular skill.

I seize this opportunity to dedicate this book to my daughters ,Iman , Rabab and Amal who have learnt English successfully according to the approach on which this book is based. Their amazing performance has made this book a reality.

I have to say that this book has to be used under the direction of a specialized teacher of English .

I do hope that this book will make it easy for the Arabs to learn English at this time when this language has become dominant in various fields of science.

The author

20th June 2006

بســم اللـه الرحمـن الرحيـم

تقـديـم وإهـداء

إن كتاب " **الإنجليزية للمبتدئين** " مصمم بالدرجة الأولى ليخدم الناطقين باللغة العربية الذين يرغبون في تعلم اللغة الإنجليزية . إن التدرج في المادة والأسلوب يتيحان للدارسين السير بيسر الأمر الذي يجعل من مهمة التعلم أمراً ميسراً.

ويركز الكتاب إلى حد كبير على الجانب الصوتي للغة بعيداً عن الطريقة القديمة التي تركز على حروف الهجاء على حساب الأصوات. وبناءً على هذا, فإن الكتاب يقدّم طرقاً لنطـق الكلمات بصورة سليمة وينتقل في سبيل ذلك من الجزء إلى الكل و يعطي مجموعـات مـن كلمات تحوي أجزاء متشابهة.

ويجدر بنا أن نقول بأن النطق السليم يـؤدي بالـدارس إلى اكتسـاب كـم مـن الكلمـات يتنامى باستمرار وهذا الأمر مرتبط ارتباطاً وثيقاً بمهارة القراءة التي إذا أحسن تطويرها فإنها يمكن أن تمهد السبيل إلى اكتساب مهارات لغوية أخرى. ولهذا فإن الكتاب يولي أهميـة كبـيرة إلى النطق السليم إضافة إلى مهارة القراءة. ولا شك في أن المتعلم الذي يمتلك مهارة صحيحة في القراءة يمكنه القيام بنواحي لغوية أخرى .

إن هذا الكتاب يتيح للدارس الفرصة لأن يمارس اللغة وذلك عن طريـق إعطـاء أنمـاط نموذجية لجملٍ وعن طريق عرض منطقي للمادة وهذا يجعل من تعلم اللغة أمراً ممتعاً.

ولقد ركزت في هذا الكتاب على وجود تكاملٍ بين جميع المهارات اللغوية دون تحيـزٍ إلى مهارة ما .

وأغتنم هذه الفرصة لكي أهـدي هـذا الكتـاب إلى بنـاتي إيمـان ورباب وأمـل اللـواتي تعلمن الإنجليزية بطريقة ناجحة حسب الطريقة التي بني عليها هذا الكتاب وكـان لأدائهـم المذهل الفضل في ظهوره .

ولا بد لي من القول بأنه يتوجب أن يكون استخدام هذا الكتاب تحت إشراف مـدرس للغة الإنجليزية .

وفي الختام أسأل اللـه العلي القدير أن يفيد هذا الكتاب أبناءنا وبناتنا في عصر أصبحت فيه الإنجليزية ا للغة السائدة في كافة مجالات العلوم الحياتية .

المؤلف إبراهيم أبو عنزة

A- **Listen** استمع

a / b / c / d / m / n / t

B - **Listen and repeat.** استمع وكرر

ba	bad	ban	bat
ca	cab	can	cat
da	dad	dam	dat
ma	mad	man	mat

C- **Listen ,repeat and learn.** استمع وكرر وأحفظ

bat   ıd سيئ   / ban

cab   / can   t

mad مجنون   / man   / mat

D- **Write the missing letters :** اكتب الحروف المفقودة

c __b   __t   b__n

ma __   / __ at   __ __

__ad   / __ __ t

٦

E- Match a word to a picture: صل كلمة مع صورة

man

cat

can

bat

cab

F- Make words : كوّن كلمات

amn : ------------ / *bac* : ---------- / *atc* : ------------

tam : ----------- / *adb* : ---------- / *amd* : ------------

G- Oral Practice   تدريب شفوي

What   is   this ?   ؟ ما هذا ؟

This   is   a --------------------.

This   is   a --------------------.

This is a ----------------------.

H- Write أكتب man   mad   mat   bat   can

_____

_____

A- Read اقـرأ :

can cab bad ban cat mad dad dam man bat

B- Match :

man

cat

bat

can

mat

C- Listen اسـتـمـع

f / g / h / k / l

D- Listen and repeat   اسـتـمـع وكرر

fa   fan   fat   fag

ga   gag   bag   bang   fang

ha   had   hand   hang   dang gang

la   lad   lag   lab   lack back black

E- Read and learn   اقـرأ وأحـفـظ

hand   / hat   / bag

bang ضربة-فرقعة   / fang   / مخلب

lad   / fan   / fat

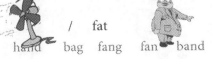

F: Write أكتب hand bag fang fan band

G- Make words : كوّن كلمات

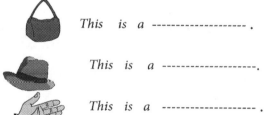

h __ __ d   /   b __ g   /   __ __ n

h __ t   /   f __ t   /   l __ d

__ at   /   __ __ m سد

H- Oral Practice تدريب شفوي :

What is this ? ما هذا ؟

This is a -------------------- .

This is a -------------------- .

This is a -------------------- .

This man is -------------------- .

This -------------- is bad.

This -------------- is bad.

This -------------- is mad.

This is a --------------- .

٩

A- **Read and match :**

fan

bag

hand

man

fang

  B- **Listen and repeat**   استـمع وكرر:

e / j / o / p

be	*bet*	*bell*	*tell*	*fell*	*jam*	*jet*	*jot*	*job*
me	*met*	*mot*	*melon* بطيخة		*pet*	*hot*	*pot*	*top*
ge	*get*	*got*	*lot*	*dot*	*pa*	*pan*	*pat*	*pet*
le	*let*	*tell*	*hell*		*eat*	*meat*	*egg*	*ebb*
ne	*net*	*neat*	*beat*		*ten*	*hen*	*den*	*pen*

bee   see   fee   feet   feel   peel

tea   team   meat   beat   heat   neat

C- **Read** اقرأ :

* *Let me go !* * *Let me tell you .*   دعني أخبـرك .

* *Let me do it for you.*   دعني أفعل لـك ذلك .

* *I can get a job.*   إني أستطيع أن أحصل على وظيفة.

* *I got a job.*   أنا حصلت على وظيفة.

 * *We get honey from a bee.*   نـحن نحصل على العسل من النحلة

* *We get money from a bank.*   نحن نحصل على المال من البنك.

* We get eggs from a hen.   ‏* We get نحن نحصل على البيض من الدجاجة.
meat from a hen.   ‏نحن نحصل على اللحم من الدجاجة .
* I can beat you.   ‏إني أستطيع أن أهزمك .
* Go to hell !   ‏اذهب إلى الجحيم.

D - Read and learn.   ‏اقرأ وأحفظ:

net   / bee   / meat

team   / tea   / jam   ‏مربى

bell   / feet

ten   / hen   t   ‏حار

E- Read and match.   ‏اقرأ وصل

meat

net

bell

tea

feet

F- Write   ‏أكتب   bell hen meat team feet fan

A- **Listen and repeat**   اسـتمـع وكـرر

q   /   u   /   r   /   s

qua *quad* quell *queen* quest *question* quit *quick*
up cup cut *hut* *nut* *fun* run sun *mum* nun
rat ran far mar park art part party cart hart
rest best lest nest rent room root loot loom
sad Sam sat set sell seem see sea seat
mask bask task mast mess best beast feast east

B- *Read and learn* اقـرأ وأحـفظ

seat / park / room

mask / sea 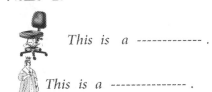 / mast

C- *Oral Practice* تدريب شفوي

What is this ? ما هـذا؟

This is a --------------- .

This is a --------------- .

This is a ------------- .

This is a --------------- .

D- **Read** اقـرأ :

I have a question for you.   Let me run for fun.
Let me have a party in a park.   We need a cart .
I need the best man.   We need rest.
We see a small bird in a nest .   Let me go to the sea .
We need a mast for the flag.   We sell honey and milk.

E- Match and learn   صل وأحفظ

queen

hut

sun

run

room

foot

F-Write the missing letters   اكتب الحروف المفقودة :

roo __ / qu __ __ n / __ un

r __ n / p __ __ k / f __ __ t

G- Make words   كوّن كلمات :

euenq : ..../ omro : ....

esat : ..../ akpr : ....

tofo : ..../ nus : ....

nahd : ..../ abg : ....

H- Write : room   seat   queen   park   mast   sun

الدرس الخامس Lesson 5

١٣

A- Read :

leg   beg   *got*   *get*   *gum*   *gun*   sun   run

beef   feet   meet   peel   see   beat   meat   neat

B- *Read and learn* اقرأ وأحـفـظ :

banana   / eat

leg   / beef

flag   / garden

C-   **Read and match** اقرأ وصل

flag

peel

eat

sea

seat

D- **Write the missing letters** اكتب الحـروف المـفـقودة:

ban __ n__   p__ __ l   /   __lag

g__ __ den   / /   __ea   /   __eg

 E- Write أكتب : banana peel flag garden beef

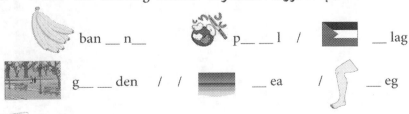

F-Oral practice تمريـن شـفـوي

What is this? مـا هـذا؟

This is a -------------- . /   *This is a ------*

This is the ----------- . /   *This is a ----------*

This is -------------- . /   *This is a ----------*

This is a -------------- . /   *This is a ---------*

G- Make words : كـوّن كلـمات

abg : .... /   dahn : ....

otof : .... /   gel : ....

dragne : .... /   nus : ....

H: *Find the word* أوجـد الكلـمة

frmeatgt /   mrebeefh /   mafanh

dnflaght /   brgardents   requeent

stbananam /   speelg   dreaty

١٥

الدرس السادس Lesson 6

A- Listen and repeat : استمع وكرر

ʋo<u>ss</u>	lo<u>ss</u>	mi<u>ss</u>	hiss	bog	log	hog	fog
big	bag	beg	bell	let	team	pool	

B- Listen and repeat : استمع وكرر

v / w / x / y / z

C- Listen and repeat : استمع وكرر

van	vast	vend	vent	vest	leave	
want	wag	wan	wet	went	west	
web	wed	well	week	weep	win	wind
wolf						
fax	lax	max	wax	box	fox	
yak	yam	yap	yard	yet	yes	you
zed	zebra	zest	zero	zigzag	zoo	zoom

D- Read and learn : اقرأ وأحفظ

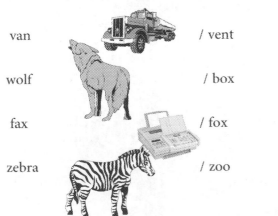

van / vent

wolf / box

fax / fox

zebra / zoo

E- Read and match: اقرأ وصل

fax

box

zoo

banana

leg

gum

صمغ

Write أكتب : box fax gum zebra wolf van

G- Find the word أوجد الكلمة

brfoxg   /   trboxrt   /   frwolfgt

derzebrads   /   hugumit /   gamantk

azzook   /   trbeefrt /   ceflagra

sevant /   mleght /   dsung

H- Read : *This is a big bag . This is a big loss. This is a hog.*
We can see a wolf , a zebra and a fox in the zoo.
Keep the gum in the box. You need beef and
honey.

Lesson 7 الدرس السابع

A- Read اقـرأ

fan	van	vest	best	beat	beast	meat
car	cat	cut	corn	creep	peak	speak

B- Read and match اقرأ وصل

leg

bag

meat

egg

jam

hand

C- Read and Learn : اقرأ وأحـفـظ

wind الريح   / window

land   / sand الرمل

band رباط   / dog

* **D- Read :** *I can speak English.*

Can you speak English ?

It is too hot. We want the best fan.

It is wet . I will have this seat.

E- Read and match : اقرأ وصل

tea

hat

park

leg

bed

F- *Write* أكتب : wind   window   sand   land   band

G- *Find the word* : أوجد الكلمة

vebedfr   reland /   sddoghs

escatr /   debandgh /   resandgr

newindeg /   ghthandel /   fewindowet

H- *Make words* : كوّن كلمات

nsu : .... /   nru : ....

dniwwo : .... /   nregda : ....

الدرس الثامن   Lesson 8

A- *Listen and repeat* : استمع وكرر

a	man	mat	bat	hat	sat
a	fake	lake	make	take	cake
	game	gate	save	cave	name
	same	plane	lane	sane	mate

 B- *Listen and repeat*

mat / mate   * **bad / bade**

fat / fate   * **hat / hate**

game - gate - name - same - tame

C- *Read and learn* : اقرأ وأحفظ

man / map   / bat

game 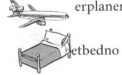 / gate   / plane

D- *Find the word* أوجد الكلمة :

 erplanert / regaterd / ntmapter

 etbedno /  remanter / regflager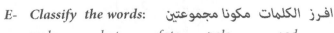

wehandqer /

 E- *Classify the words:* افرز الكلمات مكونا مجموعتين

man	male	hat	fate	pale	sad

had   name   bad   game   cat   sale

            man   pale
            bad   name

------------------   ------------------
------------------   ------------------
------------------   ------------------
------------------   ------------------

F- *Write* : hat   hate   name   game   sale   had

G- *Oral practice* تمريـن شـفوي :

What is this ?

This is a ------------- . /   This is a ----------

This is a ------------- . /   This is a ----------

This is ------------- . /   This is a ----------

الدرس التاسـع Lesson 9

A- **Read :**

٢١

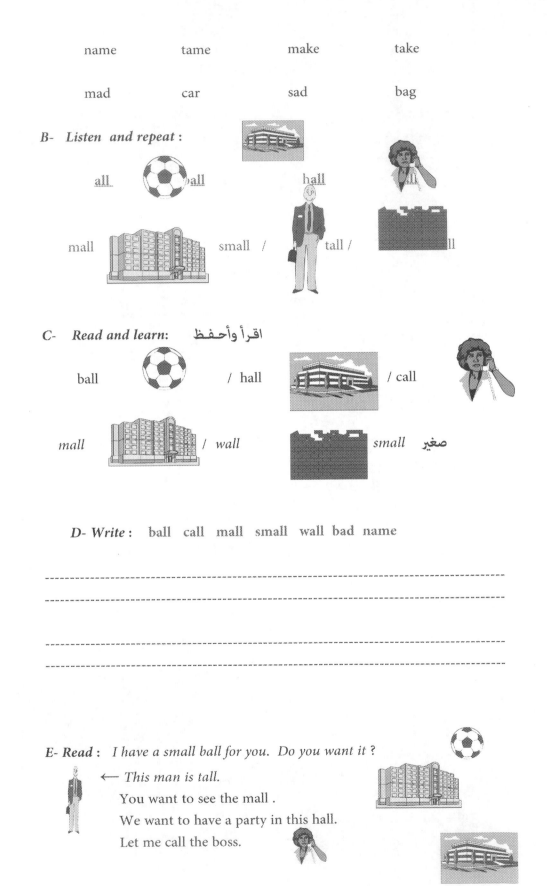

name   tame   make   take

mad   car   sad   bag

B- Listen and repeat :

all   ball   hall   ll

mall   small /   tall /   ll

C- Read and learn: اقرأ وأحـفـظ

ball   / *hall*   / *call*

mall   / *wall*   *small* صغير

D- Write : ball call mall small wall bad name

E- Read : *I have a small ball for you. Do you want it ?*

← *This man is tall.*

You want to see the mall .

We want to have a party in this hall.

Let me call the boss.

We want bananas and cakes for the party.

F- Oral practice تدريب شفوي :

What is this ?

This is a --------- ./ This is a -------------

This is a --------- ./ This is a -------------

This is a----------- ./ This is .---------------

This is the -----------. / This is -------------

G- Find the word أوجد الكلمة :

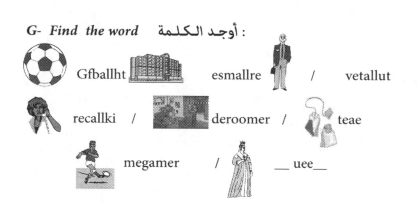

Gfballht   esmallre   /   vetallut

recallki   /   deroomer   /   teae

megamer   /   __ uee__

H- Write the missing letters :

wa __ __   /   ca __ __

sm __ __ __   /   b __ ll   g __ t __

g __ m __ / q __ een / w __ __ d __ w

الدرس العاشر 10 Lesson

A- Read and learn :

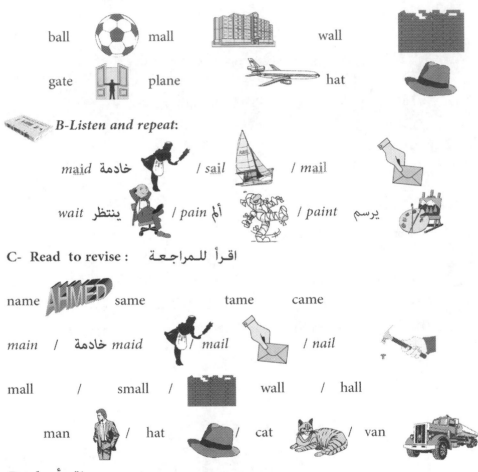

ball   mall   wall

gate   plane   hat

B-Listen and repeat:

maid خادمة / sail / mail

wait ينتظر / pain ألم / paint يرسم

C- Read to revise : اقرأ للمراجعة

name AHMED same   tame   came

main / خادمة maid / mail / nail

mall / small / wall / hall

man / hat / cat / van

Read اقرأ:

- I can make a cake. * I need a ball . * Let me go to a lake .
- *Let me take a cake to a lake. * I got a small ball.*
- I have a pain . Please ! Wait for me.
- We have a tall maid.
- Do you have an e-mail?

A- car 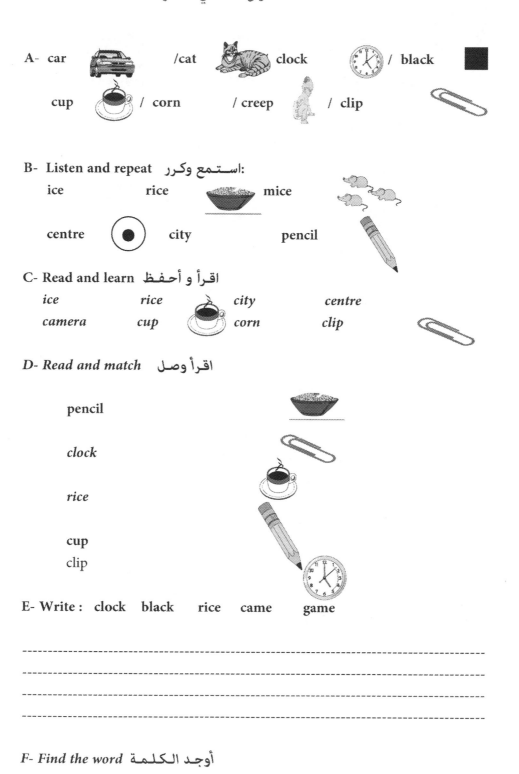 /cat clock / black

cup / corn / creep / clip

B- Listen and repeat استـمع وكرر:
ice rice mice

centre city pencil

C- Read and learn اقرأ و أحـفـظ
ice rice city centre
camera cup corn clip

D- Read and match اقرأ وصـل

pencil

clock

rice

cup
clip

E- Write : clock black rice came game

F- Find the word أوجد الكلمة

weclockre / reblackom / ewcupet

declipen / vepencilet / resricen

hecityed / focameralo / rehandef

G- Make a word : كوّن كلمـة

dsna .... / perce : ....

ternce .... / lagf : ....

eirc .... / imec : ....

licenp .... / lkcco : ....

H- Correct the word : صحح الكلمة

kween : .... / : klok : ....

maice : .... / klip : ....

kreep : .... / woll : ....

boll : .... / flak : ....

Lesson 12   الدرس الثاني عشر

A- Read :

feed   fed   keep   kept   meet   met   feel   fell
eat   beat   meat   seat   heat   tea   team   mean
peak speak leak   weak   week   keen   seek   deep

B- Listen and repeat:

i   tin / ten   pin / pen   bit / bet

        big / beg   wit / wet   list / lest

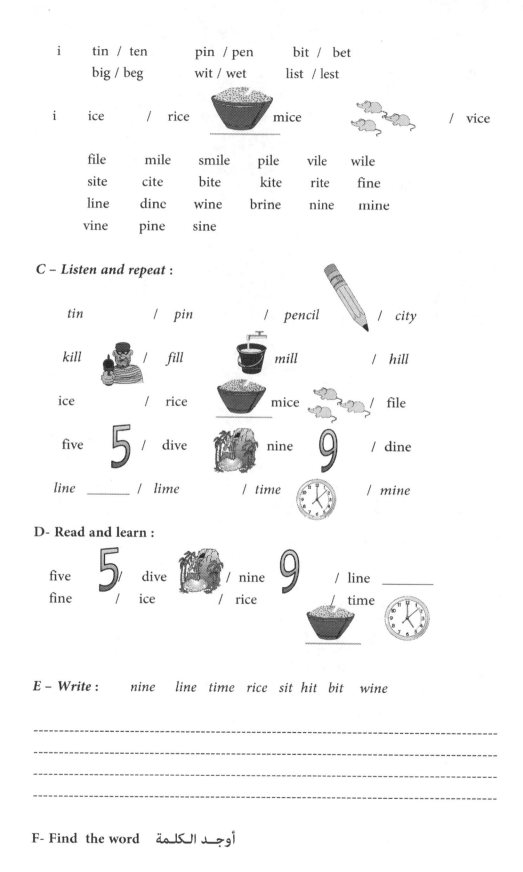

i   ice   / rice   mice   / vice

        file   mile   smile   pile   vile   wile

        site   cite   bite   kite   rite   fine

        line   dinc   wine   brine   nine   mine

        vine   pine   sine

C – Listen and repeat :

tin   / pin   / pencil   / city

kill   / fill   mill   / hill

ice   / rice   mice   / file

five   / dive   nine   / dine

line _____ / lime   / time   / mine

D- Read and learn :

five   / dive   / nine   / line _____

fine   / ice   / rice   / time

E – Write :   nine   line   time   rice   sit   hit   bit   wine

----

F- Find the word   أوجــد الكلـمة

saweekoil   / dekeeped   / deweakem

sefeedet   / wepeaked   / sespeakef

reteas   esteamoul   / edtimeou

G- Make a word كوّن كلمة:

5   evif : ....   /   eivd : ....

ienn : ....   /   einl : ....

mtei : ....   /   edb : ....

H- Oral practice تدريب شفوي

What is this ?

_____ This is a line .   /   This is rice   ....

This is a team   /   This is a pencil

What do you see ?   ماذا ترى ؟

I see -------------------- .

I see a ....

I ....

I ....

A-Read :

bit   bite   / sit   site   / spit   spite

fit   hit   mile   lime   mine   nine

B- Listen and repeat :

bi<u>r</u>d  / g<u>i</u>rl / d<u>ir</u>t وساخة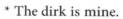

first / dirk خنجر / gird

C- Read :

* A girl got a bird.   * I hit a bird.
* We see dirt in the room.   * The dirk is mine.
* You bit me.   * The dog will bite you.

D-Read and match:

five

ten

pen

girl

nine

rice

bird

E -Write : bird girl first pencil came cup

F- Correct the word صحح الكلمة:

baird : .... /   garel : ....

dairt .... /   faive : ....

kell : .... /   clep : ....

naine : .... /   tee : ....

teem : ..../   gait : ....

C كوّن كلمة *a word* :

ribd : .... /   ilgr : ....

iemc : .... /   ridt : ....

edvi : .... /   lifl : ....

likl : ..../   klocc : ....

H- Oral practice تدريب شفوي :

What is this ?

 This is a ------------ /   *This is a ------------.*

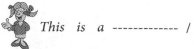 *This is a ------------./*   *This is a --------------- .*

الـدرس الرابـع Lesson 14

A- *Read* :

tin ten sit set site

hit hat / rice / line / girl

name came / milk / keep / pool

B-*Listen and repeat*:

<u>th</u> : *the* *them* *this* 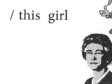 *that*
than father mother / with

th : <u>th</u>*in* *think* *thank* / *too<u>th</u>*
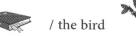 *teeth* / *three* 3 / *thrill* / *birth*

C- *Read and learn* :

the book / the bird / the meat

this book / this girl / this car

٣١

father   / mother   / tooth

teeth   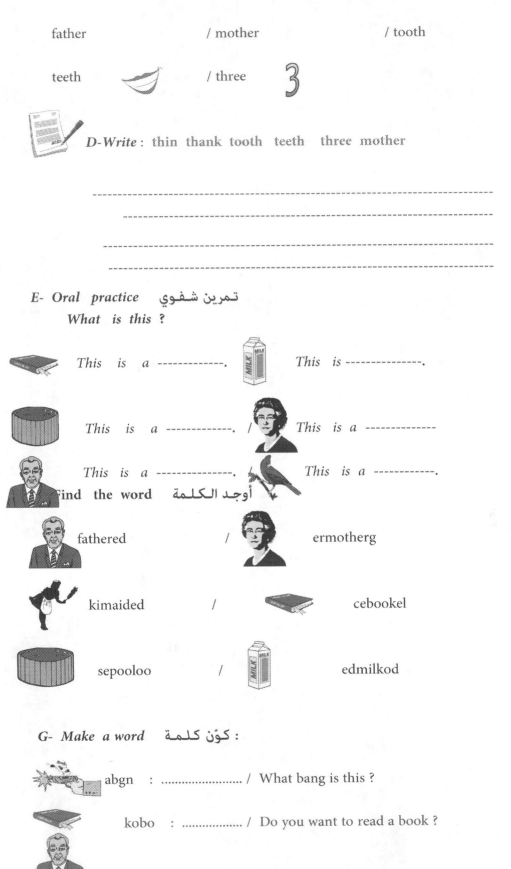   / three   3

D-Write : thin thank tooth teeth three mother

E- Oral practice   تمرين شفوي
   What is this ?

This is a ------------.   This is --------------.

This is a ------------. / This is a --------------

This is a --------------. / This is a ------------.

Find the word   أوجد الكلمة

fathered   /   ermotherg

kimaided   /   cebookel

sepooloo   /   edmilkod

G- Make a word   كوّن كلمة :

abgn : .... / What bang is this ?

kobo : .... / Do you want to read a book ?

٣٢

هـل تـريـد أن تـقـرأ كتابـاً ؟

ehtraf : .... / Do you help your father?

هـل تساعد أبيـك ؟

 thomre : .... / Does Salwa help her mother?

هـل سـلوى تـساعد أمـها ؟

الدرس الخامـس عشر Lesson 15

A- Read :

father father **this** father

mother the mother mother

tooth the tooth this tooth

* I like my father.   * I like my mother.
* The book is in the bag. * The girl is nice.
* Let me thank you   * This girl is thin.
* I can go with you.   * This tooth is bad.

 B-Listen and repeat

bird the bird this bird

nest the nest this nest

list  mist ضباب best / rest

mast last fast / cast

 C-Listen , repeat and Learn

 father / mother / tooth

٣٣

bird / girl / nest

 D-Write : list mist best last rest nest bird

الدرس السادس عشر Lesson 16

A-Read

feel   fell   keep   bet

hot / top /  moon / fool cool pool

 B- Listen and repeat

sh : **sh**ark / *sharp* حاد

ship shop

٣٤

sheep / *shed* زريبة

dish / *fish*

C- Listen , repeat and learn

ship / shop / sheep

shirt / *brush* / *fish* / *dish*

D- Oral practice تمرين شـفوي

What is this ?

This is a ----------- ./   *This is a -----------*

This is a ----------- . /   *This is a -------------*

E- Match

fish

dish

brush

girl

bird

ship

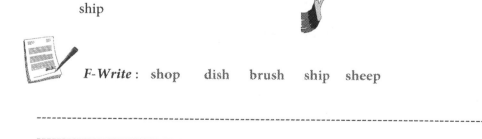

F-Write : shop   dish   brush   ship   sheep

٣٥

G- Find the word and write it   : أوجد الكلمة واكتبها

dobrushet   -------------   * Do you need this brush ?

rfishet   -------------   * We want to eat fish.

osheepefd   -------------   * I feed the sheep .

emshipod   ....   * Let me show you a ship.

vrlistad   ....   * This is a list of things
we need for the party.

modishij   ....   * I want a dish of fresh fish,
please.

H- Read

* I have a sheep .

* I need a dish.

* Let me go to the fish shop.

* They have fresh fish.

* We eat fresh fish , fresh meat and fresh eggs.

Lesson 17 الدرس السابع عشر

A-Read :

the fish   the dish   s bird

٣٦

this tooth   with   father

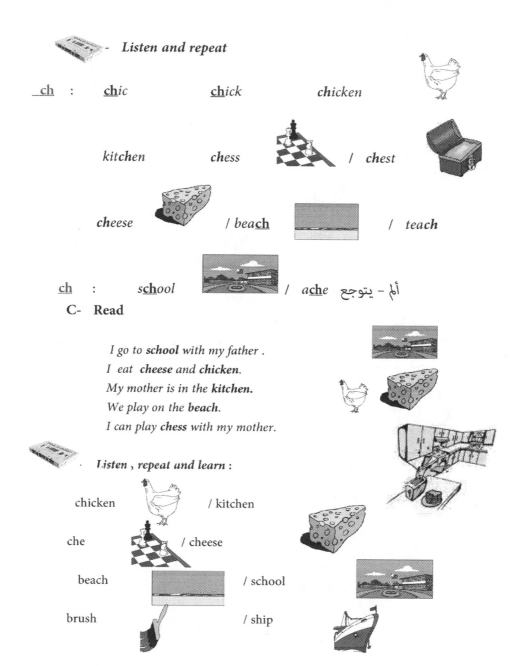

- **Listen and repeat**

__ch__ : __ch__ic   __ch__ick   **chicken**

kitchen   **chess**   / **chest**

cheese   / bea__ch__   / teach

__ch__ : s__ch__ool   / a__ch__e ألم - يتوجع

C- Read

I go to **school** with my father .
I eat **cheese** and **chicken**.
My mother is in the **kitchen.**
We play on the **beach**.
I can play **chess** with my mother.

- **Listen , repeat and learn :**

chicken   / kitchen

che   / cheese

beach   / school

brush   / ship

E- What is this ?

    This   is   a   ---------------------- .

٣٧

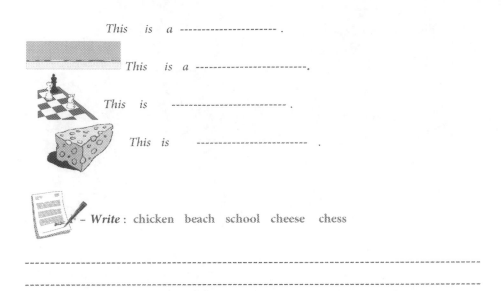

This is a --------------------- .

This is a ------------------------- .

This is ------------------------ .

This is ------------------------ .

– *Write* : chicken beach school cheese chess

G- *Choose the right word* اختر الكلمة الصحيحة :

This is (cheese - chess – ship)

This is a (chess - fish - dish)

This is a (chicken - beach – kitchen).

This is a (shop - chicken - beach).

This is a (kitchen – fish - ship).

This is a (beach - dish – ship).

H - *Read*

I need a brush to paint my room.

I see a bird on the tree.

The girl has got a small bird.

The dish is dirty. I will wash it.

My mother is in the kitchen.

She is washing a dish.

My sister is cooking fish.

I like to eat fresh fish.

We want to go to the beach.

We can swim there.

We have some chickens.

We get eggs from them.

I like to eat chicken and fish.

الـدرس الثامـن عشر Lesson 18

A-Listen and repeat :

seat   set   same   rest

case   west   list   sun

B-Listen and repeat:

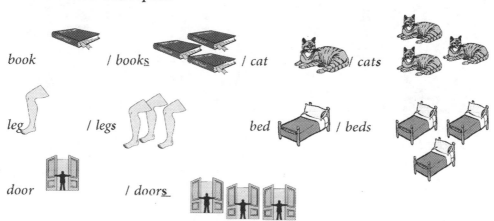

book   / book_s_   / cat   / cats

leg   / legs   bed   / beds

door   / door_s_

٣٩

rose / *ro_se_s*

 C-Listen , repeat and learn :

     book   / books   / hat      / hats

     window   / windows   / cup   / cups

     floor   / floors   / door   / doors

D-Match :

book

windows

books

ship

bag

ships

bags

 E-Write :   books   bags   ships   trees   bees

F- Oral Practice تمرين شـفوي :

What is this ?

This is a ------------ /   These are ----------

This is ------------ ./   These are --------

These are -------------- ./   This is a --------------

الدرس التاسـع عشر Lesson 19

A-Read :

kid طفل   kids   / lid غطاء   lids

room   rooms   / dog   dogs

cats   / shops   / doors   /   rose

hose   / nose   / mist   /   rest

B-Listen , repeat and learn :

h<u>ou</u>se   / houses

m<u>ou</u>se   / m<u>ou</u>th

c<u>ow</u>   / d<u>ow</u>n ↓

br<u>ow</u>n بني   / cr<u>ow</u>n

٤١

C-What is this ?

: a ------------------- .

: ------------------- .

: a ------------------- .

: ------------------- .

: ------------------- .

D-Write: house   mouse   mouth   how   now

E- Make a word كوّن كلمة

eosn : ----------------- /

seoh : ----------------/

uohes : ----------------/

sreo : -----------------------

osc : -------------------

seuom : -----------------

F- Find the word أوجد الكلمة :

hucrownert / بني *debrownse*

humouther / ↓ *dedowngt*

G- Match a word to a picture :

house

٤٢

hose

houses

mouse

nose

A- Read :

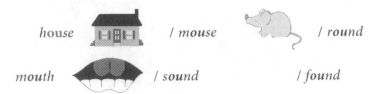

house / mouse / round

mouth / sound / found

* I have a big house .
* The table is round.
* I put a spoon in my mouth.

* I see a mouse in the house .
* I found a round table.

!- Listen , repeat and learn :

down ↓ / cow / now / how

grow / row / sow / low

flow / blow / slow / glow

C- Match a word to a picture

shirt

girl

house

rose

tooth

brush

ship

D -Write : rose hose nose tooth shirt mast

E- What is this ?

: a --------------. / This is a ------------------.

: a -------------- . / This is a ---------------- .

: a -------------- . / This is a ------------------.

: a -------------- . / This is a ------------------.

: a ---------------- . / This is a ------------------.

: a ---------------- . / This is a ------------------.

F- Choose the right word اختر الكلمة الصحيحة :

: (hose / house)

: (door / window)

: (book / books)

: (cat / cats)

: (door / doors)

: (cows / cow)

: (father / mother)

A- **Read :**

sat   bat   cat   tea   team   meat   make   take

lake   same   name   hate   rate   came   centre

 B- Listen and repeat : اقرأ وكرر

what   whet   whim   when   where

who   whose   write   wrong

 C-Listen , repeat and learn :

What is this ?

What is in it ?

Where is the book ?

Where is the boy ?

Who is in the room ?

Ali can write his name.

This is wrong .   X

Mona is wrong.   X

D- Re-order the words   أعد ترتيب الكلمات:

1- the / is / bag / Where /   : ----------------------------------- ?

2- is / Ali / Where /   : ----------------------------------- ?

3- this / What / is /   : ----------------------------------- ?

4- in / is / What/ cup/ the /: ----------------------------------- ?

5- is / in / Who / car / the /   : ----------------------------- ?

6- Can / Ali / home / go /   : ------------------------- --- ?

E-Write : Where is the book ? What can you see ?

---------------------------   --------------------------------

F- Find the word   أوجد الكلمة

erwhatr   / ewherem   / fewhoer

sehoses   / sewriteeq   / wrongef

G- Choose the right word   اختر الكلمة الصحيحة

1- (What / Where) is in the bag ?
2- (Who / Where) is in the van ?
3- I can (whose / write) my name.
4- Where is the (cat / cats) ?
5- (Where / what) is the bag ?

A-Read :

What *is this* ?   *What is that* ?

Where *is the bag* ?   *here is the father* ?

Who *is wrong* ?   *Who is sad* ?

ALI

3- Listen and repeat :

yak   yes   yet   yellow

happy   dirty   sunny   funny

my   by   cry   try

C- Listen, repeat and learn:

yak   yellow

happy   sunny   dirty
my   my book   my cat   cry

D- Write : happy dirty cry my yellow yak

E- Re-order the words   أعد ترتيب الكلمات:

1- is - Who - sad   : ----------------------------?

2- is- the -in- bag –What   : ----------------------------?

3- the - brush - Where - is : ----------------------------?

4- wrong – is - Who   : ----------------------------?

5- is - Ali - sad .   : ----------------------------.

F- What's wrong ?   ما هو الخطأ ؟

fathr : ----------------------------

mather : ----------------------------

maed : ----------------------------

shep : ----------------------------

cheep : ----------------------------

* Read :   I am happy. You are funny.
           The weather is sunny.
           I will try to fly.
           Let me try. Let me fly.
           Don't cry.

A-Read:

Where is my book ?  / Where is my father ?

The man is wrong . / The man can write it.

The girl is my sister. / My mother is happy.

B-Listen and repeat :

photo  / phone / elephant

tone / stone / bone

C-Listen , repeat and learn:

photo photos

my photo my photos

phone telephone

stone حجر bone عظم

D-What is this ?   This is a --------------------- .

This is a --------------------- .

 This is a --------------------- .

E-Write :   phone   elephant   pharmacy   plane

F- Read :

* *I go to the pharmacy with my father.*   / * *I phone my mother.*

* I ride an elephant .   / * I have a photo .

G- Choose the right word : اختر الكلمة الصحيحة

1- My mother is (bird - happy).

2- The man is (book - happy).

3- This is a (girl - sad).

4- This girl is my (sister - book).

5- This is a (phone - plane).

H- What's wrong ?   ما هو الخطأ؟ :

sester : ....

foto   : ....

fone   : ....

ston   : ....

hause : ....

wendo: ....

A- Read :

Where is my <u>ph</u>oto ?   / ... is my phone ?

What is this ?   / Who is this girl ?

The room is dirty .   / My father can write it.

B-Re-order these words أعد ترتيب هذه الكلمات :

1- is / My / dirty / shirt /   :

2- is / mother / This / my /   :

3- is / sister / wrong / My /   :

4- my / is / photo / This /   :

5- can / Ali / Hamad/ phone /   :

C-What is this ?

1-   This   is   a ----------------- .

2-   This   is   a ------------------- .

3-   This   is   a ------------------ .

4-   This   is   my ----------------- .

5-   This   is   a ------------------ .

D-Write : This is my photo . I am happy with you.

E- Choose the right word اختر الكلمة الصحيحة :

1- This   is   a   (bird - plane).

2- This   is   a   (telephone - stone).

3- The   room   is (happy - dirty)

4-.   3+2 = 4 . This is (stone - wrong)

5- This (man – girl) is my   sister.

F- Read اقـرأ :

- *Let me phone my father.*
- Show me this photo.
- I   can go to the pharmacy alone.

A- What do you see ?   ماذا تشاهد؟

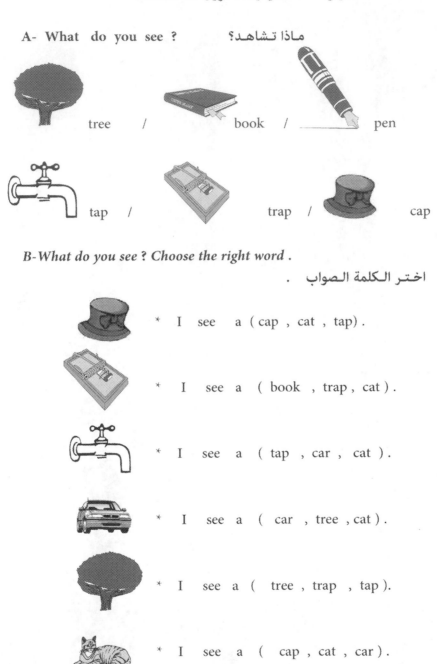

tree   /   book   /_____ pen

tap   /   trap   /   cap

B-What do you see ? Choose the right word .

اختر الكلمة الصواب .

* I   see   a (cap , cat , tap).

* I   see   a (book , trap , cat).

* I   see   a (tap , car , cat).

* I   see   a (car , tree , cat).

* I   see   a (tree , trap , tap).

* I   see   a (cap , cat , car).

C- *Match a word to a picture* . صل الكلمة مع صورتها

tap

book

trap

cap

car

cat

D-Write trap book food dog game

E- Find the word أوجد الكلمة :

metreeae / bptrap

getaper / aper

F – What's wrong ? ما هو الخطأ؟

1- pook : ....
2- tre : ....
3- ben : ....
4- trab : ....

A- Read اقرأ

 tree   free   fee   flee / bee / see

 car   can   cat / tap  / map

book   look   took / hook / cook

B- What do you see ? ماذا تشاهـد؟

 flower / fan / van

 hat / bat / seat

C- What do you see ?

1- I see a (hat , bat , seat) .

2- I see a (seat , hat , bat) .

3- I see a (bat , flower , hat) .

4- I see a (fan , flower , van) .

5- I see a (flower , fan , van) .

6- I see a (van , fan , seat).

D- Read اقرأ

I see a hat . I see a car . I see a tree .

E- Write أكتب   flower   fan   hat   tree   van

F- Write the missing letter اكتب الحروف المفقود

h__t   /   __ low __ __   /   f__n

tr__p   /   b__t   /   s__ __ t

G- Find the word أوجد الكلمة

fflowere   /   batd

meseatef   /   devane

H- What's wrong ?   ما هو الخطأ ؟

flawer : -------------------   /   *set* : -----------------------

van : -------------------./   *fan* : -----------------

٥٧

A- **Read** اقرأ

fan / van / ban / can / ran

hat / cat cap / see / sea

seat / meat / beat / flower

↓ *down* / *drown* / *brown* بـني

B- **What do you see ?** مـاذا تـرى ؟

mask / desk / cup

glass ' *grass* حشيش / *green* أخضر

C- **Match a word to a picture.** صـل الكلمة مع صورتهـا.

grass

cup

glass

mask

desk

green

أخضر

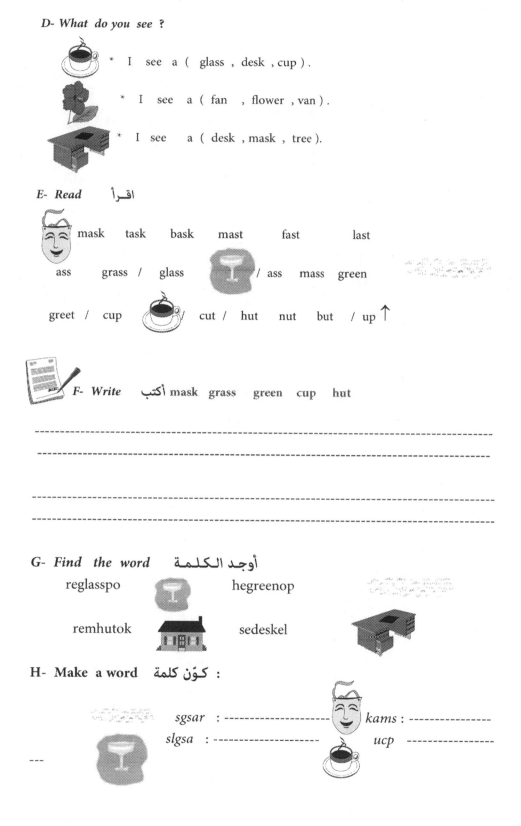

D- *What do you see ?*

* I see a (glass , desk , cup).

* I see a (fan , flower , van).

* I see a (desk , mask , tree).

E- *Read* اقـرأ

mask   task   bask   mast   fast   last

ass   grass / glass   / ass mass green

greet / cup   / cut / hut nut but / up

F- *Write* أكتب mask grass   green cup hut

G- *Find the word* أوجـد الكـلـمـة

reglasspo   hegreenop

remhutok   sedeskel

H- **Make a word** كوّن كلمة :

sgsar : -------------------   kams : ----------------

slgsa : -------------------   ucp ----------------

---

ocr ٥٩

A- *What is this ?* ما هذا ؟

rubber   number   brush
duck   mug   hut

This   is   a   ----------------------

This   is   a   ----------------------

------------   ------   ----   ----------------

------------   ------   ------   --------------

B- *Choose the right word* اختر الكلمة الصحيحة

 1-   This is a (duck – luck – suck) .

 2- This is a(hat - hut - hall) .

3- This is a (number- desk – mask) .

 4- This is a (flower – rubber – book) .

 5- This is a (rush – dish – brush) .

C- Re-order the words أعـد ترتيـب الكلمات

1- is / a / mug / This / : This ....

2- a / is / duck / This / : ....

3- a / This / hut / is /   : ....

D- Read the words : اقرأ الكلمـات

mug / rug   hug   rub / rubber / number

duck / luck / run   rush / brush

shut   / hut   cut   nut   gut   but

E- Write اكتب: rubber   number   brush   duck   mug

F- What's wrong ?   مـا هـو الخطـأ؟

mag : --------------------   hat : --------------------

hut : --------------------   rabr : --------------------

dak : --------------------   brash : ----------------

٦١

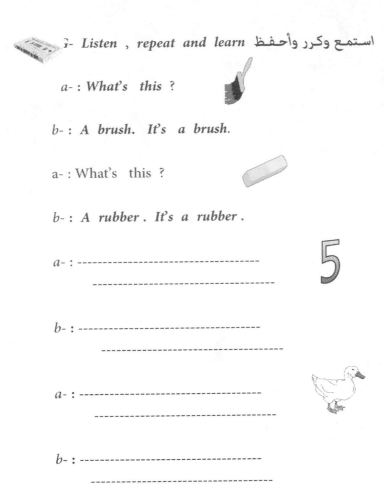

G- *Listen , repeat and learn* استمع وكرر وأحفظ

a- : **What's this ?**

b- : **A brush. It's a brush.**

a- : What's this ?

b- : **A rubber . It's a rubber .**

a- : --------------------------------
----

b- : --------------------------------
----

a- : --------------------------------
----

b- : --------------------------------

H- *Match a sentence to a picture* صل جملة مع صورة

1- I need a brush .

2- This is my duck.

3- This is my number.

4- This is my rubber.

5- The mug is on the floor.

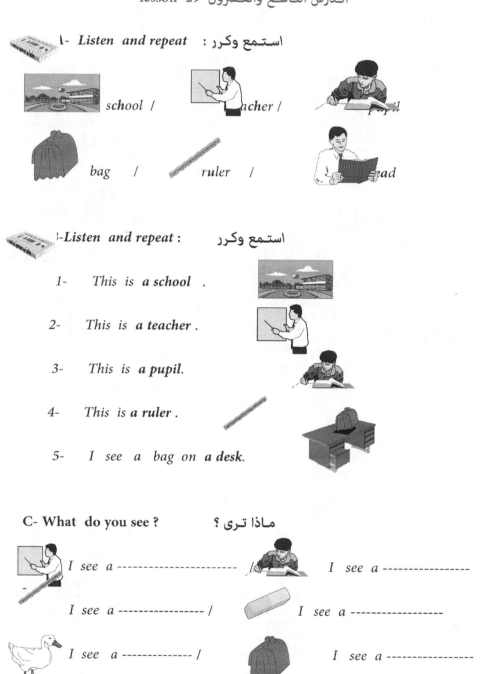

1- *Listen and repeat* : استـمع وكرر

school / acher / pupil

bag / ruler / read

\- *Listen and repeat* : استـمع وكرر

1- This is **a school** .

2- This is **a teacher** .

3- This is **a pupil**.

4- This is **a ruler** .

5- I see a bag on **a desk**.

C- **What do you see ?** ماذا تـرى ؟

I see a ------------------------ / I see a ------------------

I see a ----------------- / I see a ------------------

I see a ------------- / I see a ------------------

D- *Match a picture to a word* :   صـل الصـورة مـع كـلـمة

rubber

hut

duck

tree

teacher

E. Read   اقـرأ وافـهـم الـمـعـنـى.

This is a school . I see a teacher . I see a pupil .
The pupil is reading a book. I see a bag . I see a ruler in the bag.

F- Put (√) *or* (X)

1- This is a school.   (   )

2- I see a teacher.   (   )

3- The teacher is reading a book. (   )

4- The pupil is in the bag . (   )

5- The bag is in the ruler. (   )

الدرس الثلاثون Lesson 30

A. What is this ?

------------------ --------------- --------------- --------------- -------

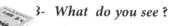
 3- **What do you see ?**   ماذا تــرى ؟

   *nurse*

hospital   *doctor*

medicine دواء   *pharmacy* /   *pain* وجع / *a cut* جرح

C- Listen and repeat :   استمع وكرر

   Mona :   I   have a cut.

   Hamad   : You can go to hospital.
   Mona   :   What can I do there ?

   Hamad   : You can see a doctor .
   Mona   :   What can he do for me ?
   Hamad   :   He can give you **medicine** .
      You can get this medicine
   at the pharmacy .

   Mona : Thank you , *Hamad. You are kind*

٦٥

D- Re-order the words اعـد ترتيـب الكلمـات

1- have / a / cut / I : ....

2- see / doctor / a / I / can /: ....

3- is / This / nurse / a / : ....

4- get / at / I / medicine / pharmacy / the :

....

E-Write : teacher   school   hospital   medicine   nurse

F-Choose the right word اختر الكلمة الصحيحة

1- I   have a (car – pain – bag) in my leg.

2- I want to see a (teacher - cow - doctor).

3- You can go to (hospital – beach - school).

4- This is (meat – milk – medicine).

5- This is a (photo – phone – pharmacy) .

G- What's wrong ? مـا الخطـأ؟

hospitel : ..../ medecin ....

farmasy : .... / nars ....

٦٦

الدرس الحادي والثلاثون Lesson 31

A- What do you see ? ماذا تــرى ؟

fish / dish / rubbish

 ship / shop / sheep

B- What is this ?

1- It is a (fish - dish – sheep).

2- It is a (shop - ship - sheep).

3- *It is (dish - rubbish_ - ship).*

4- It is a (rubbish - ship - sheep).

5- It is a (fish - ship - shop).

 C- Listen and repeat : استمـع وكرر

1- I go to a shop to buy a dish .

2- I go to a fish shop to buy fish.

3- I have a sheep . I feed it .

4- I see rubbish. This is bad .

٦٧

D-Listen . and answer :   استمع وأجب

1- What do you have ?

   I have a ....

2- What do you do ?   ماذا تفعل؟

   I .... my sheep.

3-Where do you go ?   أين تذهب؟

   I go to the ....

4- Why do you go there ?   لماذا تذهب إلى هناك؟

   To .... a dish .

5- Where do you go ?

   I go to the sea .   إني أذهب إلى البحر.

6-Why do you go there ?

   To see a ....

E-Write :   I go to a shop to buy a dish .

F-Choose the right word :   اختر الكلمة الصحيحة :

   1- I feed my (ship - shop - sheep).

   2- I go to a (shop - book - ruler).

الدرس الثاني والثلاثون Lesson 32

A- Listen and repeat : استـمـع وكـرر :

1- What do you need ?   ماذا تحتاج؟
   I need a ....

2- Why do you need it ?   لماذا تحتاج إليه؟ / it = chair /
   I .... it to sit on.
   To sit on .   لكي أجلس عليه.

3- What do you sit on ?   على ماذا تجلس؟
   I .... on a ....

4- Where do you sit ?   أين تجلس؟
   ....

B- Listen and learn :   استـمـع وأحـفـظ :

You أنت / I أنا / sit يجلس / on على / buy يشتري / feed يطعم

C-Re-order the words   أعد ترتيب الكلمات

1- sit / on / chair / I / a /: ....

2- need / chair / a / You/ : ....

3- go / I / a / to / shop / : ....

4- fish/ buy / You/ : ....

D- Write the missing word اكتب الكلمة المـفـقودة

1- I .... on a chair.
2- I have a ....
3- You .... fish.
4- You sit on a ....
5- I go to the shop to .... a dish.
6- You go .... the shop to buy ....

E- Read and learn :

I **need** a chair **to sit on** .

You **sit on a chair.**

I go to the shop **to buy fish.**

I **need** you.

You need **a teacher.**

I need **a doctor.**

You go **to the pharmacy** to get **medicine** .

٧٠

F -Listen and answer : استمع وأجب

1- *Why do you go to   hospital ?   To* ....

2- *Why do you go to the pharmacy ?* ....

3- *Why do you go to the shop ?* ....

4- *Why do you need a book ?* ....

5- *Why do you need money* نقود *?* ....

G-Write a word under each picture أكتب كلمة تحت كل صورة :

-----------------------   -----------------------   -----------------------

-----------------------   -----------------------   -----------------------

A-Listen and repeat : استمع وكرر

thief لص   tooth   teeth   three

throat   thorn الشوك   thin نحيف

throne

B-Listen and learn the words : استمع وأحفظ هذه الكلمات

he هو → = Ali , Hamad , doctor , teacher

it هو - هي- انه- إنها → = cat , book , car , chair

my لي → my book كتابي/ my car سيارتي/

your لك -لك / your book كتابك/ your car سيارتك/

C- What do you see ?

: I see a ....

: I see a ....

: I see a ....

D-Listen and repeat :

1- I clean my teeth . I need a brush to clean my teeth.

2- You need a brush to clean your teeth.

3- I see a doctor .   He is thin.

4- I see a thief .   He is bad.

5- I see a duck .   It is big.

E- Listen and answer: استمع وأجب
What do you need ?

I   need a ....

2- Why do you need it ?   لماذا تحتاجها؟
To .... *my* ....

3- Where is the cat ?
It is .... *the car* .

4- Where is the bird ?   أين الطائر ؟
.... *the cage.* (القفص)

F- Read

my throat   / your throat / my tooth / my teeth

your teeth / throne   / thorn   / three

D-Put " this " or " these " :

1- **This** is an ant . **These** are ants.

3- ------------ is a cat.   4- ------------ is a duck.

5- ------------ are ducks .   6- ------------ is a girl.

7- -------------- are trees.   8- ------------ is a bag

E-Put " is " or " are "

1- This .... an apple.   2- These ....ants.

3- These .... cats.   4- This .... a doctor.

5- This .... a duck.   6- These .... ducks.

F-Match a sentence to a picture   صل جملة مع صورة مناسبة.

1- This is a teacher .

2- These are books.

3- This is a fish .

4- These are dogs.

G- **What is this ?**

It's an .... /   It's an ....

· This is an ..../   : This is a ....

A-Re-order the words أعد ترتيب الكلمات

1- need / a / car / I / : ------------------------------------

2- is / This / book / my/ : ------------------------------------

3- is / bag / your / This / : ------------------------------------

4- have / apple / I / an / : ------------------------------------

5- eat / egg / an/ I : ------------------------------------

B-Listen and repeat

1- **This** is **a** tree .   هذه شجرة →

This is a book.   →هذا كتاب.

This is an apple .   هذه تفاحة . →

This is an ant .   هذه نملة. →

2- **These** are trees.   →هذه أشجار.

These are books.   هذه كتب. →

These are apples.   هذه تفاحات. →

C- Put " a " or " an "

1- I have -------- book .   2-You have -------- bag.

3-I need -------- car   4- You eat -------- apple.

5- I see -------- egg .   6- It is -------- elephant.

D-Put " this " or " these " :

1- **This** is an ant .

2- **These** are ants.

3- -------- is a cat .

4- -------- is a duck.

5- -------- are ducks .

6- -------- is a girl.

7- -------- are trees.

8- -------- is a bag

الـدرس الـسـادس والثلاثون Lesson 36

A-Capital letters : حروف كبيرة

$a \rightarrow A$ / $b \rightarrow B$ / $c \rightarrow C$ / $d \rightarrow D$ / $e \rightarrow E$ / $f \rightarrow F$

B- Write capital letters : A   B   C   D   E   F

C-Match a small letter to a capital one: صل حرف صغير مع أخر كبير.

d   F

a   E

b   D

f   C

e   B

c   A

D- *Listen and repeat . Colours*   الألوان

green   أخضـر / *red*   أحمـر / *black*   أسود / *white*   أبيض

blue   أزرق /   *yellow*   أصفر / *brown*   بـني

E-Match a word to a colour .   صـل كـلمة مـع اللون المناسب .

green   أصفر

black   أبيض

white   أسود

yellow   أخضر

   F. Ask a question :   اسـأل سـؤالاً

a. what colour is the car ?

b. It's black .

1- What ----------------------------- ? It is green .

2- ------------------------------ ------- ? *It is brown.*

3- ------------------------------ ------- ? *It is blue.*

4- What ----------------------------- ? *It is black .*

G- Read

I can see a car . It is your car . It is blue and brown.

This is my car. It is white .

I have a red rubber and a black pencil.

الدرس السابع والثلاثون Lesson 37

 A ۰۰۰- *Listen and repeat*

1-Where is <u>the book</u> ?

↓

It is <u>on the table</u>. انـه على الطاولة.

2- *What colour is it ? It is ----------------.*

3- Where is <u>the ball ?</u>

↓

It ---------------- <u>under the car.</u> إنها تحت السيارة

4- *What colour is it ? It is ---------------- and ------------*

5- Where is Ali ?

↓

He is <u>in the car</u> . انـه في السيارة.

6- Where is Mona ?

↓

She is <u>in</u> the car . إنـها في السيارة.

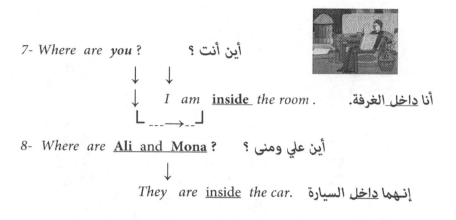

7- Where are **you** ?　　　أين أنت ؟

　　　↓　　↓

　　　↓　　I am **inside** the room .　　أنا <u>داخل</u> الغرفة.

　　　└ --- → -- ┘

8- Where are <u>Ali and Mona</u> ?　أين علي ومنى ؟

　　　　　　　↓

　　　They are <u>inside</u> the car.　إنهما <u>داخل</u> السيارة

9- Where are <u>the **apples**</u> ?

　　　　　　↓

　　　They　are　**in a basket**　<u>on a table</u> .

B- Answer

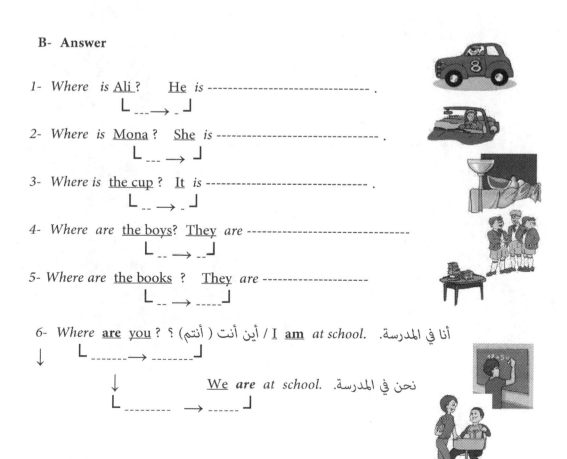

1- Where is <u>Ali</u> ?　　He is ---------------------------------- .

　　　　└ --- → - ┘

2- Where is <u>Mona</u> ?　She is ---------------------------------- .

　　　　└ --- → ┘

3- Where is <u>the cup</u> ?　It is ---------------------------------- .

　　　　└ -- → - ┘

4- Where are <u>the boys</u>?　They are ----------------------------------

　　　　└ -- → -- ┘

5- Where are <u>the books</u> ?　They are --------------------

　　　　└ -- → ----- ┘

6- Where **are** you ? ؟ أين أنت (أنتم) / I **am** at school. أنا في المدرسة.

↓　　└ ------- → ------- ┘

　　↓　　　　<u>We</u> **are** at school. نحن في المدرسة.

　　└ --------- → ------ ┘

٧٩

C- Ask and answer :

Ali : ....?

Mona: On the table. It's on the table.

Ali : ----------------------------------?

Mona: In the bag . They are in the bag .

Ali : ----------------------------------?

Mona : He is inside the car.

Ali : ----------------------------------?

Mona: They are under the tree .

Ali : ----------------------------------?

Mona : I am in the room.

D- Put a suitable word ضع الكلمة المناسبة :

1- The ruler is ---------------- the bag.

2- The books are ---------------- the table.

3- Hamad is ---------------- the car .

4- The boys are in the ----------------.

5- I am ---------------- a tree.

E- Find the word   أوجد الكلمة

1- recoloures : ----------------   2- oundere : --------------------

3- dehes   : ----------------   4- fosher   : ----------------

5- sotheyew   : ---------------   6- fesead   : ----------------

الدرس الثامن والثلاثون Lesson 38

A- Read :

I need <u>this apple</u>.   <u>It</u> *is red.*

└--- --- → ------┘

These are <u>apples</u>.   <u>They</u> *are red.*

└------- → ----------┘

B- Capital letters :

g → G / h → H / i → I / j → J / k → K / l → L /

C-Match a small letter to a capital one : صل حرف صغير مع أخر كبير.

b	G
d	I
g	B
h	D
i	H

D-Listen , repeat and learn : استمع وكرر وأحفظ

father

mother

زوج **husband**

زوجة *wife*

daughter ابنة

ابن *son*

 E-*Listen and repeat:* استمع وكرر:

I   am   Ali Nasser . s is my family.   هذه أسرتي.

This is my wife , Noura.

This is my son, Hamad.

This is my daughter , Mona.

F- Tick (√) *or* (X) :

1- Ali is the father.   (   )

2- Mona is the mother.   (   )

3- Hamad is the son.   (   )

4- Noura is the daughter.   (   )

G- *Find the word and write it* أوجد الكلمة ثم أكتبها :

1- *fefatherd* : ----------------

2- *notmotheres* : ----------------

3- *morson* : ----------------

4- *wifero* : ----------------

5- *sdaughter* : ----------------

6- *fethroated* : ----------------

7- *queenor* : ----------------

8- *reteethes* : ----------------

9- *wemediciner* : ----------------

10- *gorfeedes* : ----------------

الدرس التاسع والثلاثون Lesson 39

 ۱-Listen and repeat :   استمع وكرر

* *Whose book is this ?*  كتاب من هذا ؟

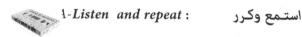

Pupil a :   Mine . It's mine. انه لي . It's my book. انه كتابي.

Pupil b :   Yours. لك . It's yours. انه لك. It's your book. انه كتابك

Pupil c :   It's Ali's . . انه لعلي . It's Ali's book. انه كتاب علي.

Pupil d :   No . لا . It's not Ali's. انه ليس لعلي.
It's Mona's .
I know it's Mona's . إني أعرف انه لمنى.

B- Look at the picture and say whose it is: انظر إلى الصورة وقل لمن هذا.

1- It's ----------------- .

2- It's ----------------- .

3- It's ----------------- .

C- Learn :

* This is my book.   هذا كتابي لي. / This book is mine.

     It's mine.   انه لي.

     This is your book.   هذا كتابك./ It's yours.   انه لك.

      This is Ali's car.   هذه سيارة علي/ It is his car.   إنها سيارته.

     It's his.   إنها له.

This is Mona's ring.   هذا خاتم منى.

    It's her ring.   انه خاتمها.

    It's hers.

D- Put " my , mine , your , yours , his , her , hers" :

1- This is ------------- book .   It's ------------- .

   It's not ------------- .

2- This is Ali's bag .   It's ------------- bag.

3- Mona is ------------- sister. This is ------------- pen.

4- Ali is Mona's father . This is ------------- book.

5- This is my mother. This ring is ------------- .

E – Put a possessive in each space: ضع كلمة تدل على الملكية في كل فراغ

1- It's ------------- cat.

2- It's ------------- cat.

3- It's ------------ cat.

4- It's ------------- cat .

F- Re-order these words أعـد تـرتيب الكلمات:

1- your / This / book / is : --

2- Ali's / is / This / house : ---------------------------------------

3- is / duck / mine / This : ---------------------------------------

الـدرس الأربـعـون Lesson 40

A- Listen and answer : استـمع وأجب

1- Whose room is this ?   * It's ------------------ .

2- Whose bed is this ?   * It's -------------------- .

3- Whose pen is this ?   * It's -------------------- .

4- Whose car is this ?   * It's -------------------- .

B- Listen and repeat :

Whose <u>books</u> *are these ?*   كتب من هذه؟

↓

They are mine.   إنها لي.

They're yours.   إنها لك.

They're Ali's .   إنها لعلي.

They're Mona's.   إنها لمنى.

C- Learn :

* *It is* ⟶ *It's* .   * *They are* ⟶ *They're* .
* *This is* **my book.**   * *These are* **your books** .
* *It is* **his bed.**   * *They are* **my books.**

D- Choose the correct word : اختر الكلمة الصحيحة

1- This (are – is) my car.

2 - This is your (car - cars) .

3- *These* (is – *are*) *his cats.*

4- These are her (book – books).

5- It (is – are) an apple.

6- *This* (*is* – *are*) *an egg.*

7- They (is – are) my sisters.

8- They are your (book – books).

9- This car is (my – mine).

E- Correct what's wrong : صحح الخطأ

1- *This apple is him .*   (   ) -----------------

2- *This bag is my.*   (   ) -----------------

3- *This is you bag.*   (   ) -----------------

4- *It's not yours bag.*   (   ) -----------------

5- These is my fingers.　　　(　　) ------------------

6- It's an bag.　　　　　　　(　　) ------------------

7 These are her book.　　　 (　　) ------------------

8 These are mine books.　　 (　　) ------------------

9- They is his sisters.　　　 (　　) ------------------

F- Fill in the spaces:　　أملأ الـفـراغ

his　　book　yours　book　　her　　hers　　my

1- This is -------- sister, Mona. This is ------- ring.

2- This ball is ------------------ .

3- This ------------------ is yours.

3- Ali is my brother. علي أخي /　This is ------------- bag.

4- These ------------------ are mine.

5- This bag is ------------------ . It's not mine.

الـدرس الحـادي و الأربـعـون　Lesson 41

١- **Listen and repeat :**

Who is this man ?  من هذا الرجل؟

Who is this girl ? من هذه الفتاه؟

B-Read and answer:　اقـرأ وأجـب

I am Jassim . This is my family. Noura is my wife (زوجتي).

I have a boy. His name is Hamad. I have a girl.

Her name is Mona.

1- Tick (√) or (X) :

a- Jassim is the father.   (   )

b- Noura is the mother.   (   )

c- Hamad is the father.   (   )

d- Mona is the girl.   (   )

2- Who is the father ?   ----------------------------

3-   Who is the mother ?   ----------------------------

4- Who is Mona's brother ?   ----------------------------

5- Who is Mona's father ?   ----------------------------

C- Fill in the spaces   أملأ الـفـراغـات :

father   sister   mother   brother   wife   girl

1- Jassim has عنده a -------------. Her name is Mona.

2- Who is Jassim's ----------------------?

3- Mona is Hamad's ----------------------.

4- Jassim is Mona's   -------------------.

5- Noura is Hamad's   -------------------.

6- Hamad is Mona's   -------------------.

D- Re-order the words : أعـد ترتيب الكلمات

1- my / is / father / This/   ------------------------------------

2- bag / This / yours/ is /   --

3- are / his/ These / books/ -----------------------------------

4- have / a / I / car/   -------------------------------------

5- is / Jassim/ father/ Mona's/ ---------------------------------

E- Find the word   أوجد الكلمة :

   1- nefatheres   2- lemotherop   3- tersisteref

   4- dbrotherea   5- rogirlas   6- wowifed

F- Correct what's wrong   صحح الخطأ :

1- ander : ------------ 2- brawn : ------------ 3- garl : ----------

4- bluo : ---------- 5- gren : -------------- 6- mather: -------

الدرس الثاني والأربعون 42 Lesson

A: Listen and repeat :

I **have** a book .   Ali **has** a car .

↓   ↓

أملك-عندي   يملك-عنده

* I **have got** a book . → I've got a book. (يملك-لدي have got)

* Ali **has got** a car . → Ali's got a car. (يملك-لديه has got)

B-Listen and repeat :

1- What have you got ?   ماذا لديك؟

   I've got a car.

2- What have you got ?
   I've got a ----------------.

3- What has Ali got ?   ماذا لدى علي؟

He has got a ----------------.

He's got a boat.

4- What has Mona got ?

She's got a ----------------.

C- Put " have " or " has " :

1- Ali ---------------- got a green bag.

2- Mona ---------------- got a red car.

3- I ---------------- got a blue bag.

4- You ---------------- got black hair.

D-   Correct what is wrong صحح الخطأ :

1- They has got a small house. --------------------------------

2- Mona have got black hair. --------------------------------

3- Ali have got a small boat. --------------------------------

4- I have get a green carpet.   --------------------------------

5- This are a red car.   --------------------------------------

E- Ask a question : اسأل سؤالا

1- Who is Jassim ?

2- -------- --------- Mona ?

3- -------- -------- Hamad ?

4- ---------- -------- Noura ?

5- ----------   ------- Mona's father?

6- -----------   ------- Hamad's sister ?

7- Who ------------   -----------------------?

F- **Fill in the spaces with these words**   أملأ الفـراغ :

have   has   is   this   these   who   whose

1- ---------------- is this girl ? / 2- I ------------- got a red car.
3- ---------------- is my house . / 4-Your house ------- green .
5- ---------------- is this bag ?
6- Hamad ---------------- got a green bag.
7- ---------------- are my books.

G- **Ask a question:** اسأل سؤالا

1-What have you got ?

2- ------------   ----------   you ------------?

3- -----------   -----------   ----------   got ?

4- What ----------- Mona got ?

5- What ----------- Hamad ----------- ?

6- What --------- he -----------?

7- ------------   --------- she ----------- ?

٩١

H- Ask and answer :

Pupil A : Who is Jassim ?

Pupil B : He's Hamad's father.

Pupil A : What have you got ?

Pupil B : I've got a -------------- .

Pupil A : Who is Mona's brother ?

Pupil B : ---------------- is .

Pupil A : What has he got ?

Pupil B : He's -------- a ---------------------------- .

Pupil A : Who is Hamad's sister ?

Pupil B : --- .

الدرس الثالث والأربعون 43 Lesson

A-Capital letters : حروف كبيرة

$$m \rightarrow M \ / \ n \rightarrow N \ / o \rightarrow O \ / p \rightarrow P \ /$$

$$q \rightarrow Q \ / \ r \rightarrow R \ / s \rightarrow S$$

B- Answer : أجب

1- What has Ali got ? * ---------------------------- .

2- Where is it ? * -------------------------------- .

3- What colour is it ? * ---------------------------- .

4- What have you got ?* ------------------------------.

5- Whose girl is Mona ?* ------------------------ .

C -Match a small letter to a capital one :

g   Q

h   B

d   R

p   G

b   H

r   D

q   P

D- Choose the correct word :

1- This (are – is) my leg.
2- These (is - are) your trees.
3- I (have – has) got a small car.
4- Ali (have- has) got a red car.
5-These (book- books) are mine.

E - Learn to say the numbers. Listen and repeat . تعلّم الأرقام

1 (finger) 2 3 / 4 5

one (1) / two (2)/ three (3) / four (4) / five (5)

F- Match a number to a word : صل الرقم مع الكلمة المناسبة

3	two
4	five
1	three
5	one
2	four

G- How many books ... ?   كم كتاب.........؟

1- How many books have you got ?

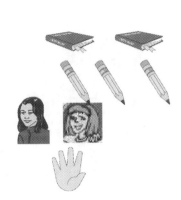

2- *How many pencils has Ali got ?*

3- How many sisters have you got ?

4- How many fingers do you see ?

H- Write full answers :   أكتب إجابات كاملـة

1- How many cars do you see ?

I see ----------------------------------

2- How many boys do you see ?

--- .

3-How many girls do you see ?

--- .

4-How many sisters have you got ?

I have ----------- ----------- ----------------------

5- How many pencils have you got ?

--- .

6- How many brothers has Ali got ?

He (= Ali) has ----------- ----------- *brothers.*

7- How many apples has Mona got ?

She ----------- -------------- ----------- --------------

I- *Re-order these words* : أعـد ترتيب الكلمات
1- many / got / books / How / you/ have /
--- ?

2- has / red / She / car / a / got /

الـدرس الرابع والأربعون   Lesson 44

A- Oral practice   تـدريـب شـفـوي:

1- *How many apples have you got ?*
2- Where are they ?
3- What colour are they ?

٩٥

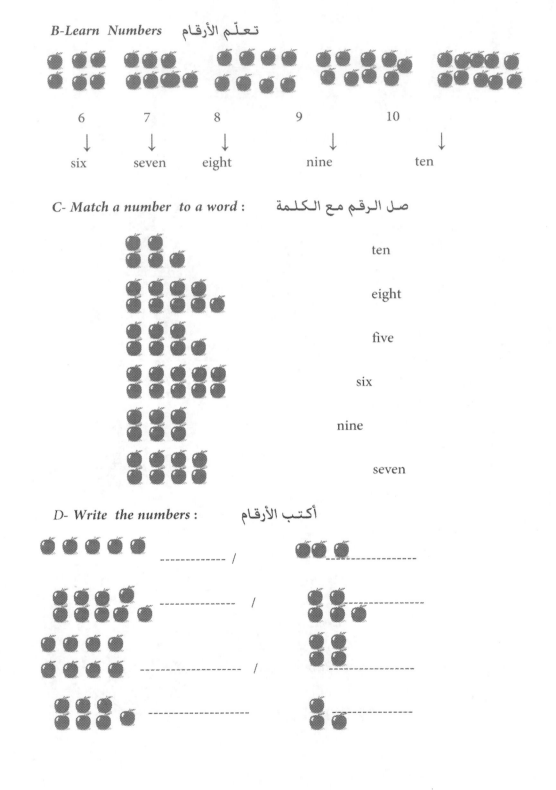

B-Learn Numbers   تعلّم الأرقام

6	7	8	9	10
↓	↓	↓	↓	↓
six	seven	eight	nine	ten

C- Match a number to a word :   صل الرقم مع الكلمة

ten

eight

five

six

nine

seven

D- Write the numbers :   أكتب الأرقام

----------- /

-------------- /

-------------- /

E- Read and write the number : اقرأ واكتب الـرقم

three : -------------- eight : --------------

seven: -------------- ten : --------------

five : -------------- one : --------------

two : -------------- four : --------------

nine : -------------- six : --------------

F- Capital letters : حـروف كبـيـرة

$t \rightarrow T$ / $u \rightarrow U$ / $v \rightarrow V$ / $w \rightarrow W$

$x \rightarrow X$ / $y \rightarrow Y$ / $z \rightarrow Z$

G-_Match a small letter to a capital one: صل حرف صغير مع حرف كبير

t	R
v	D
x	B
u	T
b	X
d	V
r	U

H- Write the small letter :   أكتب الحرف الصغير

B : -----------/ D : -------------/ G : ------------/ A : ------------

R : ----------/ Q : ------------/ U : ----------/ F : -------------

H : ----------/ I : ----------/ L : -----------/ J : -------------

I- Learn   numbers : تعلّم الأرقام

11 (10 + 1 = 11) / 12 (10 + 2 = 12) / 13 (10+3)
↓   ↓   ↓
eleven   twelve   thirteen

14 (10 + 4)   /   15 (10 + 5)   / 16 (10 +6)
↓   ↓   ↓
fourteen   fifteen   sixteen

J - Read and write the numbers : اقرأ واكتب الأرقام

ten   : -------------/ *five*   : ------------/ *fifteen* : -------------
nine   : -------------/ *sixteen* : -----------/ *eleven* : -------------
twelve : -------------/ *fourteen* : -----------/ *four*   : ------------
seven : -------------/ *three*   : ------------/ *thirteen* : -------------

I-Answer : أجب

1- *How many books have you got ?*

Three books .

2- How many pencils has Ali got ?

3- How many birds do you see ?

4- How many boys do you see ?

5- How many ducks are there ?

K- Make words كوّن كلـمات :

1- esnev: -------------/ 2- veif : -----------/ 3- rfuo: --------------

4- xsi : ------------/ 5- gieth: -----------/ 6- owt : --------------

7- eno : -----------/ 8- rtehe: ----------/ 9- etn : ----------------

L- Correct what's wrong صحح الخطأ:

1- faive : -------------/ 2- thre : -------------/ 3- cix : -------------

4- sven : ------------/5- nain : ----------- / 6- fuor : -----------

7- haw : ------------/ 8- mainy : --------- / 9- dack : -----------

A- Write the missing numbers : أكتب الأرقام المفقودة

1   2 ------   4 ----   6   7 ----- ------- -------

11   ------ 13 ------ -------   16 ----- ------ 19

¦- Listen , read and answer : استمع واقرأ وأجب

*I am Ali . **I have got** three boys . I have got five girls.*

*I **live in** a small **house in the city** of Doha . We have six*

*rooms : three **bedrooms** , **two bathrooms and a kitchen.***

house   / bedroom   bathroom

kitchen   / city

* Tick (√) or (X) :

1- Ali lives in a small house.   (   )

2- Ali has got five boys.   (   )

3- Ali has got three girls.   (   )

4- Ali lives in Doha.   (   )

5- Doha is a city .   (   )

١٠٠

* *Answer* :

    1- How many rooms are there ? --------------------------

    2- How many bedrooms are there ?------------------------

    3- How many bathrooms are there ?------------------------

    4- Where does Ali live ? -------------------------------

    5- How many boys has he got ? -------------------------

C-- Answer these questions :   أجـب على الأسـئـلـة

    1- How many balls do you want ?   كم كرة تريد؟

                    ↓

              I want five balls.

    2- How many pencils do you need ?

    3- How many apples do you see ?

D- Re-order the words   أعـد ترتيب الكلمات :

    1-   have / three / got / eggs / I /

    2-   has / two / She / pencils / got/ :

    3-   want / apple / an / I :

    4-   live / in / city / a / I :

    5-   are / rooms / four / There :

- **Listen and repeat** :

How much **milk** do you want ?

How much **cheese** do you want ?

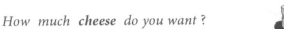

3- **Listen , repeat and learn** :   استمع وكرر وأحفظ

milk / tea / salt eat

cheese sugar r

water money ffee /

C- **Note** : لاحـظ

books , cars , pens , boys , trees ⟶ (√)

tea (√) , *teas* (X) , **milk** (√) , *milks* (X) , *butters* (X) ,

sugars (X) , **breads** (X) , **meats** (X) , **moneys** (X)

* How many pencils .... ? (√)

* How many sugar .... ? (X)

* How much sugar .... ? (√)

١٠٢

D-Listen and answer :

1- How many books do you have ? _____ books.

2- How much tea do you want ?

A kilo . (a cup , a little قليلا ,)

3- How much cheese do you want ?

4- How much butter do you want ?

------------------------------------- three pieces . ثلاث قطع

5- How much money do you need ?

------------------------------- 10 riyals.

6- How much sugar do you want ?

------------------------------- 2 spoonfuls. ملئ ملعقتين

E- **Choose the right word** اختر الكلمة الصحيحة :

1- How (many - much) books do you have ?

2- How (much – many) cheese do you want ?

3- I want five (egg – eggs).

4- I need a kilo of (meat - meats).

5- He wants a cup of (teas – tea).

6- I see three (boys – boy).

7- She (have - has) got a ball.

8- How many (milk – ducks) are there ?

9- How much (milk – milks) do you want ?

10- There are five (pencil – pencils).

A- Read and tick (√) or (x) :

1- **How much tea** do you want ? (   )

2- How many sugar do you want ? (   )

3- How much money do you want ?(   )

4- **How many cars** do you see ? (   )

5- I need a kilo of meat. (   )

6- I has got a little oil. (   )

7- Ali have got much money. (   )

8- I have got many pencils. (   )

B- What is the weather الجو **like** ? ما حالة الجو؟

* *It's sunny* . إنه مشمس. *cloudy* . إنه مغيم.

It's too hot. إنه حار جدا

* *It's rainy.* إنه ممطر s too cold. إنه بارد جدا.

It's raining. الدنيا تمطر *It's snowing.* إن الدنيا تسقط ثلوجاً

C - What do you <u>have to</u> do ?   مـاذا يجب أن تـفـعـل؟

يجب

* I   have to use my sunshade.

شمسيتي-مظلتي / أستخدم

 -------------- <u>wear</u> <u>heavy</u> <u>clothes</u>.

ملابس   ثقيلة   ألبس

* I -------------- *use my umbrella.*

* I -------------- -------------- *my raincoat.*

* I -------------- *switch on my A/C .*

* I -------------- *see my doctor.*

D- Oral Practice   تـدريـب شـفـوي :

What do you do ?   مـاذا تـفـعـل؟

1- It's too cold .   / 2- It's too hot .

3- It's rainy .   / 4- It's sunny.

E- Match a sentence from A with a sentence from B :

<u>A</u>	<u>B</u>
1- I am ill .	( ) I wear heavy clothes.
2- It's sunny .	( ) I've to use my umbrella .
3- It's too cold.	( ) I see my doctor.
4- It's rainy.	( ) I have to switch on the A / C.
5- It's too hot.	( ) I use my sunshade.

A- Listen and repeat :

Pupil A : **How are you ? How do you do ?** كيف حالك؟

Pupil B : <u>I'm</u> *very well , thank you.* إني بخير .شكراً لك.

↓

I am very well, thank you.

Puil A : *How is <u>Ali</u> ?*

↓ ↓

Pupil B : ↓ *He is very well .*

└ → ┘

Pupil A : *How is <u>Mona</u> ?*

↓

Pupil B : *She is sad.* إنها حزينة.

Pupil A : *How are <u>your friends</u> ?* كيف حال أصدقائك؟

↓ ↓

Pupil B : ↓ <u>They are</u> *happy.* إنهم سعداء

└ --- → ------- ┘

↓

<u>They're</u> *happy.*

B -Learn :

I am . → *I'm.* / * *He is.* → *He's.* / * *She is.* → *She's .* / *You are.*
→ *You're ./ We are* → *we're.* /*They are.* → *They're./*

C -Write the short form اختصر

I am happy. ----------------------. / *He is sad.* --------------------
She is well. ---------------------- / *You are ill.* ---------------------
We are late. --------------------- / *They are lazy* ------------------

D- How are these people? Listen and repeat :

1- This boy is scared. مرعوب

2- ---------------------------- is ill.

3- This ------------- ---------- tidy. نظيف

4- ------------ boy ------------ untidy.

5- --------- ----------- --------- lazy. كسول

6- ---------- ----------- ------- sad. حزين

7- ---------- ---------- ---------- kind. حنون

E -Put " am , is , are" in the spaces:

1- Ali ------- tidy , but ولكن you ----------- untidy.

2- I ---------- happy , but Ali ---------- sad .

3- She --------- sad , but I --------happy .

4- We -----------kind.

5- My father -------------- kind to me.

6- My mother ----------- tidy , but Mona is ------------.

7- My sisters ---------- kind to me ,but you -------------
   unkind .

F- Choose the right word :

1- I am (happy - tidy - scared).

2- He is (sad - happy - lazy).

3- He is (sunny - ill - kind).

4- The weather is (sunny – cloudy – rainy).

5- I have to use my (kind- raincoat- umbrella).

G -Ask and answer : اسأل وأجـب

A : Is Ali happy ?

B : Yes , he is.

A : Is Hamad kind ?

B : *Yes, ------------------ .*

A : Is Mona tidy ?

B : *Yes , ------------- .*

A : *---------- your ------------------------- kind ?*

B : *------------- , ------------- ------------- .*

A : *---------- your father --------------------- ?*

B : *------------- , ------------- ------------- .*

H- Match a picture to a sentence :

1- This boy is untidy.

( ) - This boy is scared .

3- This boy is tidy.

( )

4- They are sad .

( ) 5- This man is ill.

6- We are happy .

مـلاحظة :

تعتبر هذه الكلمات صفات *sad- happy- tidy – sunny- hot – cold rainy*

ويتم استخدامها مع فعل خاص بـها وهو : *am/ is / are* / على النحو التالي :

* I am happy.

* Ali (= he /Mona =she) is tidy.

* The car is red.

* We are happy .

* You are happy.

* They are sad.

A - Use " not" : ضع الجمل في النفي

1- Ali is ------- ill. / 2- I'm -------- free./ 3- You are ------ busy.

4- Mona and Ali are -------- tidy.   / 5- We are -------- free.

B- Ask a question: اسأل سؤالاً

1- ------ Ali tidy ? / 2- Is Ali ---------? / 3- ------ Mona free?

4- --------- you -------------? / 5- ------------ the boys at home?

6- ---------- your books ------------- the bag   ?

7- ---------- your bag -------------- the table?

8- -------------- you OK ?

C- Listen ,repeat and practise :

A :	Is Ali ill ?	هل علي مريض ؟
B :	No , he isn't. He's OK.	كلا. إنه ليس مريضاً. إنه بخير.
A :	Is he in the kitchen ?	هل هو في المطبخ؟
B :	No, he isn't.	كلا. إنه ليس في المطبخ.
	He's in his room.	إنه في غرفته.
A :	Is your sister busy ?	هل أختك مشغولة؟
B :	No. She is free.	
A :	Are you free ?	
B :	No. I'm busy.	كلا. إني مشغول.

A :   Are your brothers tidy ?   هل إخوتك مرتبون؟

B :   No, they aren't.

        They're untidy.   إنهم ليسوا مرتبين.

A :   Is your car small ?

    B :   No, it isn't. It is big.

      A :   Is it red ?   هل هي حمراء؟

      B :   No, it isn't. It's green.   كلا .إنها خضراء.

الدرس الخمسون Lesson 50

A-Listen and repeat :

*   ***What do you do in the morning ?***   ماذا تفعل في الصباح ؟

*I **get up** at five o'clock.*   *ash .*

*I **pray** in the mosque .*   *I **have** breakfast at home.*

*I **change** my clothes   I **go** to school at seven.*

B- Listen and understand : استمع وافهم

A : **What** do you do <u>in the morning</u> ? → في الصباح
B : **I get up** at five.

A : What do you do next ?
B : **I wash** and **pray**.

A : **Where** do you pray ?
B : **In the mosque.**

A : **Where** do you have breakfast ?
B : **At home.** في البيت

A : **When** do you have breakfast ?
B : **At 6:30** .

A : **What** do you have for breakfast ?
B : Jam , butter , cheese , milk , bread and eggs.

A : **How** do you go to school ?
B : **By bus.**

C-Answer the questions: أجب على الأسئلة.

1- **When do you get up ?** ---------------------------

2- *Where do you pray ?* ----------------------------------

3- <u>**What time**</u> *do you* <u>*have*</u> *breakfast ?*

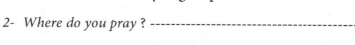

في أي وقت / ↓ / تتناول / طعام الإفطار /

I have -------------------------------.

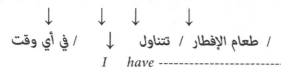

١١١

4- What do you have for breakfast ?

     I have --

5- How كيف do you go to school ?

     I go by -------------------------------.

D-Re-order the words : أعـد ترتيـب الكلمات

1- *at / get/ o'clock / I / up / five* : --------------------------- .

2- *the / I / mosque / pray / in* :--------------------------- .

3- *have / milk / breakfast / I / for* : ---------------------

4- *go / at / home /o'clock / one / I* : ---------------------

E- **Find the word**   أوجـد الكـلمة :

  1- remorninged   / 2- wwashrt   / 3- seprayet

  4- kechangeas   / 5- jebreakfastop   / 6- nomosqueer

F- **Write :**

    I change my clothes . I have breakfast at home.

G- **Correct the mistakes**   صحـح الأخـطـاء :

    1- I git ap at six in the morning.

    2-   I prey in the mosqe .

    3-   I need my ambrella.

A- **Listen , repeat and learn** :

** <u>What</u> *do* <u>you</u> <u>do</u> <u>in the afternoon</u> ?

بعد الظهر   تفعل   أنت   ماذا

** ***What do you do in the afternoon ?***

*I **get back** home at on:*   *have lunch .*

*I **take** a rest .*   *I **do** my homework.*

*I **play** football .*   *I **watch** TV .*

 3- **Listen and repeat** :

A : *When do you* <u>go home</u>   تعود إلى البيت؟
B : *At one.*

A : <u>Where</u> *do you* <u>have</u> <u>lunch</u> ?

أين   تتناول   طعام الغداء
Where do you have lunch ?
B : *At home.*   في البيت

١١٣

A : <u>What</u> do you have for lunch ?

↓

ماذا

B : <u>Rice</u> , <u>meat</u> , <u>salad</u> and <u>fruit</u> .

↓   ↓   ↓   ↓

الأرز   لحم   سلطة   فاكهة

A : What do you <u>do</u> <u>after lunch</u> ?

↓   ↓

بعد الغداء / تفعل

B : I take a rest .

أخذ قسطاً من الراحة.

A : What do you do <u>after that</u> ?   ماذا تفعل بعد ذلك ؟

↓

بعد ذلك

B : <u>I</u> <u>do</u> <u>my homework</u> .

↓ ↓   ↓

أنا أعمل   وظيفتي المـنـزلية

I <u>play</u>   <u>football</u> .

↓   ↓

ألعب   كرة القدم

I <u>watch</u> <u>TV</u> .

↓   ↓

أشاهد / التلفاز

C- **Write the missing word** : أكتب الكـلـمـة الـمفـقـودة

1- What --------- you --------- in the afternoon ?

2- What do ---------- do in the afternoon ?

3- What do you --------- in the --------------------- ?

I -------------- home.   I --------------------- lunch.

I take a -------------- . I do my -------------------- .

I play -------------- .   I ------------------- TV.

١١٤

D- Put the words into the correct order :

1-   have / home / I / at / lunch /

2-   my / do / homework / I /

- --

3-   watch / home / TV / at / I /

4-   in / play / the / football / garden / I /

E- Choose the right word اختر الكلمة الصحيحة:

1- I have (duck – book - breakfast) at home.
2- I (play - watch – pray) in the mosque.
3- I go (in – to – on) school .
4- I do my (lunch – father- homework) .
5- I play football in the (bedroom - garden – kitchen).

F- Correct what's wrong : صحح ما هو خطأ
1- lanch   : ---------------   2- sheese : ---------------

3- bred   : ---------------   4- frot : ---------------

5- watsh   : ---------------   6- moske : ---------------

7- rect   : ---------------   8- homewark : ---------------

9- moring : ---------------   10- raice : ---------------

A- Listen and repeat :

A : *Do you go to school ?*
B : Yes , I do .

هل تذهب إلى المدرسة :

A : Do you play football ?
B : Yes , I do .

A : *Do you drink coffee ?*
B : No , I don't.

هل تشرب القهوة ؟

A : *Do you have lunch at school*
B : No, I don't.

هل تتناول الغداء في المدرسة؟

3- Listen and answer :   استمع وأجب.

A : Do you watch TV ?

B; ------------------------------

A : *Do you play football* in the bedroom ?   في غرفة النوم
B : ------------------------------

A: Do you do your homework ?
B: ------------------------------

A :   Do you have meat for breakfast ?
B : ------------------------------

قاعدة :

نستعين بـ *do* في حالة تكوين سؤال في وجود أفعال مثل *play - have – eat- drink*

أمثلة :   * You play football

هل تلعب كرة القدم؟   *Do* you play football ?

ماذا تلعب ؟ ← I play football.   What **do** you play ?

أين تلعب ؟ ← I play in the garden.   Where **do** you play ?

متى تلعب ؟ ← I play in the afternoon.   When do you play ?

C- Ask questions:

1- -------------- you go to school ?

2- -------------- you play football ?

3- Do you -------------- TV ?

4- ----------- ---------- pray ?

5- Where -------- you pray ?

6- Where --------- you --------- lunch ?

7- ------------ ---------- you go home ?

8- What -------- ----------- play ?

9- Where --------- ----------- play football ?

10- ---------- you -------------- a rest ?

11- When ----------- you take --------------?

12- What ----------- you ----------- after lunch ?

ملاحظة :

* نستعين بـ (*don't*) ومعناها (لا) في حالة نفي أفعال مثل: *do- go- play- eat – pray*

have –   أمثلة:

أني لا ألعب في غرفة نومي.   * I **don't** play in my bedroom .

أنت لا تصلي في المسجد.   * You **don't** pray in the mosque .

نحن لا نتناول طعام الغداء في المدرسة We **don't** have lunch at school

الأولاد لا يأتون بواسطة السيارة.   * The boys **don't** come by car.

إنهم (إنهن) لا يشربون الحليب.   * They **don't** drink milk .

١١٧

D- Make the following negative : استخدم النفي:

1- You get up at six.

2- My sisters play football.

3- Ali and Mona go to the park.

4- I have lunch at school.

5- We watch TV .

E- Put the words into the correct order .

1- in/ pray/ Do/ the / mosque/ you/ :

2- school/ to/ you/ Do/ go / :

3- your / TV/ Do/ sisters/ watch/ :

4- you/ When/ go home / do / :

5- do/ pray/ Where/ you/ :

6- don't/ TV/ watch/ I / :

7- by / don't / We / bus/ come / :

F- *Write a sentence under each picture :* أكتب جملة تحت الصورة

----------------------------------   ----------------------------

-----------------------------   -------------------------------- ------------------

الدرس الثالث والخمسون Lesson 53
* Things we eat . أشياء نـأكلـها *

 A: **Things we have for breakfast :** أشياء نتناولها في الفطور

bread   honey عسل   jam

butter   se   ok il

eggs

 B: *Things we have for lunch :* أشياء نتناولها في الغداء

rice   / meat   / fish

vegetables   / salad   / yogurt

sweets   / *fruit* فاكهة   / bread

١١٩

Listen and repeat:

A : What do you have **for breakfast** ?
B : **Bread , honey and cheese**.
A: Do you have jam ?
B : Yes, I do.
A: Do you have **fish for breakfast** ?
B: Fish for breakfast ? Oh , no !
A: Do you have **butter for lunch** ?
B : No, I don't . I don't have butter for lunch.
    I have butter for breakfast.

D- Answer the questions :

1- What do you have for lunch ?

2- Do you have meat for lunch?

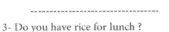

3- Do you have rice for lunch ?

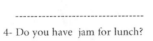

4- Do you have jam for lunch?

5-What do you have for breakfast ?

E- Put (√) or (**X**) :

1- Do you have jam for breakfast ?   (   )
2- I not have honey for lunch.   (   )
3- We don't have butter lunch.   (   )
4- Where you have lunch ?   (   )
5- When do you get up ?   (   )

F- Make sentences : اصنع جملاً

1- rest / after lunch / : ------------------------------

2- school / bus /   : ------------------------------

3- pray / mosque /   : ------------------------------

   . football / garden / : ------------------------------

5- homework / home / : ------------------------------

6- eggs / breakfast / : ------------------------------

الدرس الرابع والخمسون Lesson 54

How do you eat ?   كيف تأكل ؟

A- Listen and repeat:

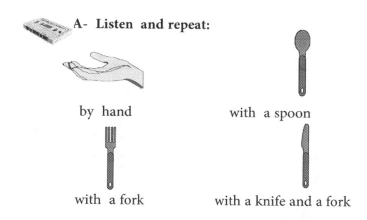

by hand   with a spoon

with a fork   with a knife and a fork

B-Listen :

A :   Do you eat rice ?

B :   Yes, I do.

A: *How do you eat <u>it</u> ?* (*it = rice*)

B :   **By hand.**

         I eat rice by hand.

A : Do you eat yogurt?

B : Yes, I do . I like <u>it</u> so much.

.

A : How do you eat <u>it</u> ?   (it = yogurt)

B : **With a spoon** . I eat it with a spoon .

A : What do you have for <u>supper</u> ?   وجبة العشاء

B : <u>roast chicken</u>.   لحم دجاج مشوي

A : How do you eat <u>it</u> ?   (it = roast chicken)

B : **With a knife and a fork.**

C: Fill in the space :

1- I eat rice by -------------------------

2- We eat yogurt with a ----------------

3- They don't eat fish with a ------------

4- You eat roast meat and --------------------.

D- Ask a question : اسأل سؤالاً

1- How do you --------------- rice ?

2- How ----------- ------------ ------------ roast fish ?

3- --------------- -------------- you eat yogurt ?

4- ------------- --------------- --------------- eat the salad ?

5- ------------- ------------ you eat an apple ?

E: Put into the correct order :

1- hand/ eat/ by / a banana / I / :

2- yogurt/spoon /eat/a /with/You/:

3- eat/ with / meat/ They/ fork/ a/ :

4- with/ cut/We/ a knife/ meat/ :

F- Find the word أوجد الكلمة :

1- deknifeeo / 2- geforkes / - spooner

 4- gohandrg / 5- opyogurt 6- gefruity

G- Correct what's wrong صحح الخطأ:

1- spon : --------------- 2- nife : ---------------

3- yagart : --------------- 4- frot : ---------------

5- forc : --------------- 6- eet : ---------------

7- battr : --------------- 8- haney : ---------------

9- shicken: --------------- 10- shange: ---------------

الدرس الخامس والخمسون Lesson 55
What do you need ... ? ماذا تحتاج؟

A- *Listen and repeat* :

Ali : What do you need to eat yogurt ?

Mona: **Of course , a spoon.** I need a spoon.

Ali : But I need **a knife and a fork** .

Mona: Why do you need <u>them</u> ? → a knife and a fork.

Ali : <u>To eat</u> roast chicken. → لكي أكل

Mona: OK. <u>I'll bring you</u> a knife and a fork. → إني سأحضر لك

Ali   :   Mona, how can I eat the yogurt ?

Mona: OK . I'll get you a spoon. ← .حسناً.إني سأحضر لك ملعقة

Ali: Mona, don't forget. I need a spoon , a knife and a fork.

لا تنسى ↓

Mona: I know. I'll get them soon.   سوف أحضرها في الحال.

Ali   :   Thank you, Mona.

  B-Listen and learn :

feed يطعم - يغذي / cut يقطع / buy يشتري

write يكتب / drive يقود-يسوق / ride (دراجة-حيوان)يركب

  C- Listen and answer :

Ali :   What do you want , Mona ?   ماذا تريدين يا منى ؟

Mona: I want **some** meat, please.

↓   ↓

بعضاً من   من فضلك

Ali :   Why ? → لماذا
Mona: **To feed** my cat.   لكي أطعم

I want to feed my cat .   إني أريد أن أطعم قطتي.

It's hungry.

Ali :   But we don't have any meat.

Do you have money ?

Mona: Yes. I have ten Riyals.

١٢٤

Ali :   *I need this money.*

I need it to buy meat for your cat.

Mona: <u>Here you are</u> . **<u>Run to the shop</u>** !

↓   ↓

أركض إلى الدكان   هذا ما تريد

D- Put (√) or (X) :

a- Mona wants some meat.   (   )
b- Mona is hungry.   (   )
c- Ali wants some meat.   (   )
d- They don't have meat.   (   )
e- Mona wants to feed her horse. (   )
f- Mona has got ten Riyals.   (   )
g- Ali runs to the shop to buy apples. (   )

E- Listen and answer :

a-   Why does Mona need meat?
     To --- .
     Because لأن *her cat* ------- --------------------- .

b-   Why do you want bread and cheese ?

     Because I --------- --------------------- .

c-   Why does Ali need money ?

     To لكي --- .

d-   Why do you need a knife ?

١٢٥

e-   Why do you need a pen ?

----

f-   Why do you want a car ?

--- *home.*

g-   Why does Hamad want a horse ?

--- .

h-   Why does Ali run to the shop ?

--- .

F- Find the word :

1- rerunn   2- nobuyet   3- erfeedtr

4- wecutre   5- deshopre   6- gedriveh

7- fewritemg   8- wehungryed   9- fohoneyur

G- *Write a word under the picture* أكتب كلمة تحت الصورة

-------------- -------------- -------------- -------------- --------------

-------------- -------------- -------------- --------------   --------------

١٢٦

I don't play .... / Do you play...... ?

Ali doesn't play..... / Does Hamad play...?

 A- listen and repeat :

I play football.

I don't play basketball.

You play football , but you don't play basketball.

We drive to school , but they don't drive there.

 B- Listen and repeat :

a- **Do** *you play football ?*

b- **Yes, I do.**

a- **Do** *we have money ?*

b- **No , you don't.**

a- **Do** *they drive to school ?*

b- **Yes , they do.**

a- *Where* **do** *you buy meat ?*

b- *I buy meat at the shop.*

a- *Why* **do** *they need money ?*

b- *They need it to buy some books.*

*قاعدة: في حالة وجود الضمائر I - you - we - they
أو أسماء تمثلها مع أفعال مثل :

play - need - want - run - eat - drive

فإننا نستخدم *do* في حالة السؤال أو *don't* في حالة النفي كما في الأمثلة السابقة.

١٢٧

C: **Listen and repeat :**

Ali plays football , but he **doesn't** play basketball.

Mona needs meat , but she **doesn't** need money.

Hamad **goes** to school, but he **doesn't** go to the park.

 - **Listen and repeat :**

a- **Does** Mona need meat for her cat ?

b- Yes, she **does.**

a- What does Ali need ?

b- He needs money.

a- **Does** he need a horse ?

b- **No, he doesn't.**   He only wants money.

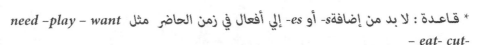

* قاعدة : لا بد من إضافة-s أو -es إلي أفعال في زمن الحاضر مثل want – play– need
- cut– eat -

إذا كان معها ضمائر مثل   he - she – it أو أي اسم ينوب عنها.

نستعين بـ does في حالة السؤال أو doesn't في حالة النفي مع أفعالٍ مثل الأفعال السابقة وفي وجود الضمائر السابقة أيضاً. أنظر إلى الأمثلة السابقة.

E- Choose the correct answer :

1- I (need – needs) a car.
2- Ali (want- wants) a knife to cut the meat.
3- Mona (want – wants) some meat to (feed – feeds) the cat.
4- We (don't – doesn't) play in the garden.
5- They (plays- play) football in the garden.
6- (Do- Does) you go to school ?
7- (Do- Does) Ali need money ?
8- Does Mona (want – wants) meat ?
9- Where (do- does) she go ?
10- What (do- does) you have for lunch ?

F- Correct what is wrong :

a- Ali need money.   (   ) -----------------
b- I feeds my horse.   (   ) -----------------
c- I not like milk   (   ) -----------------
d- Mona like milk.   (   ) -----------------
e- Mona don't play football.   (   ) -----------------
f- Does you need this book ?   (   ) -----------------
g- What you eat in the morning ?   (   ) -----------------
h- She go home by car   (   ) -----------------
i- He do his homework at home.   (   ) -----------------
J- Mona have a car.   (   ) -----------------

G- Choose the right answer اختـر الإجابة الصحيحة

1- Do you play football ?
  a- Yes , you do .   b- Yes, I don't.   c- Yes, I do.

2- Does Mona need a car ?
  a- Yes , he does.   b- Yes, she does.   c- Yes , I does.

3- How do you eat rice ?
  a- by hand .   b- in hand .   c- at hand .

٨- Listen and repeat :

a : What do <u>you</u> <u>want to</u> <u>do</u> ?

b :   ↓   ↓   ↓

I want to **ride** my horse.

I want to **write** *a letter.*

I want to **feed** my camel.

I want to **wash** my hands.

I want to **play** football.

B- Answer the questions :أجـب على الأسـئلـة

* **What do you want to do ?**

1 - (have my lunch): ---
2- (watch TV) : ---
3- (buy a ball) : ---
4- (climb a tree) : ---
5- (write a letter) : ---

C- Learn how to answer a question: تعلّم كيفية الإجابة على سؤال

What does Hamad want   to do ?
        ↓   ↓   ↓
    He   wants to go home.

What does Mona want to do ?

↓   ↓   ↓

She wants to go shopping. تذهب للتسوق

Answer :

1- What do you want to do ?

I ---

2- What does Ali want to do ?

He ---

3- What does Noura want to do ?

She ---

4-What does your mother want to do?(wash dishes)

5- Where does your sister want to play ?

--- .

6- What do your friends أصدقاؤك want to do?(go fishing)
They ---

D-Put into the correct order :

1- want / drink / I / milk / to/
--- .

2- to / wants / Ali / green/ car/ buy / a /
--- .

3- father / ride / wants / horse / his /to / My /
--- .

4- don't / play/ want / football / I / to /

   -- .

5- go fishing / want / doesn't/ Ali / to /

   -- .

E- Choose the right word   :اختـر الكلمة الصحيحة

1- I want to (pray – wash) my hands.

2- Ali (want – wants) to play football .

3- *My father wants to (buy – climb) a car.*

4- *My mother wants to (watch – wash) TV.*

5- *My brothers (want – wants) to go fishing.*

F- Find the word   : أوجد الكلمة

1- hrideo   2- ewriten   3- krfeedb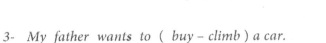

4- foplayes   declimbre   fishinge

G- Write a word under the picture أكتب كلمة تحت الصورة :

---------------   --------------------   ----------------------   ---------------

What will you do ?   ماذا سوف تفعل؟

   A- Listen :

Noura   :   Ali , I don't have a pen.

Hamad   :   * <u>Don't worry</u> . *I'll give you one.*   * لا تقلقي

Noura   :   *And the homework is* *<u>difficult</u>.   * صعب

Hamad   :   Don't worry. I'll * help you.   * يساعد

Noura   :   *When will Dad* *<u>get back</u> ?   * يعود

Hamad   :   *He'll* *<u>be back</u> +<u>soon</u>.   * يعود / + قريباً

* عندما نريد أن نعمل شيئا في المستقبل فإننا نستخدم هذه الجمل :

* *I* <u>**will go**</u> *to school* <u>**tomorrow.**</u>

    ↓   ↓

سوف أذهب   غداً

* *I* <u>**will feed**</u> *my horse* <u>**soon**</u>.

* Hamad **will** wash the car **soon**.

* *She'll* *<u>**make**</u> *a cake* <u>**soon**</u>.   تصنع كعكة

*للاختصار فإننا نستخدم

* *I'll go .* ⟶ *I will go.*

* *He'll do the homework.* ⟶ *He will do the homework.*

   B- What will you do ?

a- *Your brother is ill* مريض .

----

    b- You are late for school . متأخر عن المدرسة

----

c- Your room is not tidy. غير منظمة

------------------------------------. (*tidy it* **up** يرتبها)

١٣٣

C- Choose the right word :

a- I (am - have- will) see my friends tomorrow.
b- She'll (wash – watch – washing) the dishes.
c- I'll (plays- play) football with Hamad.
d- They (are - will – have) buy a car soon.

D- Put into the right order :

a-   will / my/ wash / car/ soon/ I /

--- .

b-   feed / cat / will / her / soon / She /

--- .

c-   tomorrow / will / shopping / go / We /

--- .

E- Answer the questions   أجب على الأسئلة:

a- Where will you play football ?

   I will play ---------------------------- .

b- What will you buy   ?

--- .

c- When will you buy it ?

--- .

d- Who will you go fishing with ?   مع من سوف تذهب للصيد ؟

--- .

What can you do ? ماذا تستطيع أن تفعل ؟

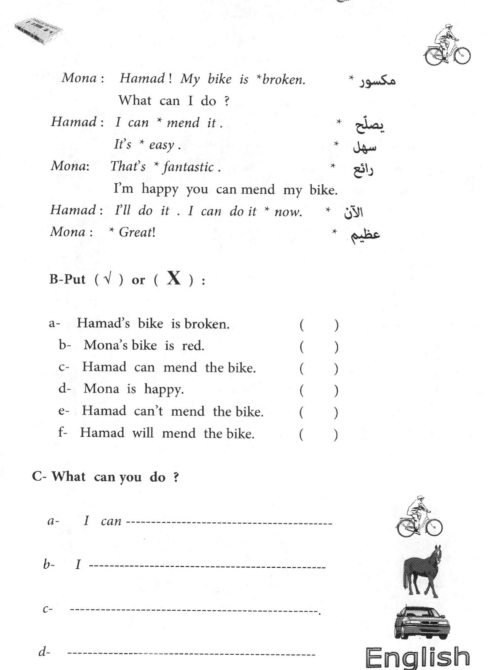

Mona :   Hamad ! My bike is *broken.   * مكسور
         What can I do ?
Hamad : I can * mend it .   * يصلّح
         It's * easy .   * سهل
Mona: That's * fantastic .   * رائع
         I'm happy you can mend my bike.
Hamad : I'll do it . I can do it * now.   * الآن
Mona :   * Great!   * عظيم

B-Put (√) or (X) :

a- Hamad's bike is broken.   (   )
 b- Mona's bike is red.   (   )
 c- Hamad can mend the bike.   (   )
 d- Mona is happy.   (   )
 e- Hamad can't mend the bike. (   )
 f- Hamad will mend the bike.   (   )

C- What can you do ?

a-   I can -------------------------------------

b-   I --

c-   --.

d-   --

English

١٣٥

D- Listen :

a-   Can you do * everything ?   * كل شيء

b-   No , I can't . I can't do everything.

  * But I can do <u>some things</u>. بعض الأشياء / *   ولكن

a-   What can you do ?

b-   I can swim . I can play football.

  I can eat and drink.

a-   Can you buy a big car ?

b-   No, I can't.

  I can't buy a car .

  I don't have * a lot of money .   * كثيراً من المال

E- Listen and answer :

a- Can you climb a* high * mountain ?

    * عالٍ   *   جبل

--- .

b- Can you drive a tractor ?

--- .

c- Can you * jump off this tree ?   * يقفز من

--- .

d- Can you write English ?

--- .

F-Write what you can do . أكتب ما تستطيع أن تفعله

a- --- (ride)

b- --- (sing a song أغني أغنية)

c- --- (mend)

d- --- (use the computer)

G- Write things you can't do :

a- I can't -------------------------------- (*drive*)

b- I -- (*dive* أغوص)

c- I -- (أطير بطائرة *fly a plane*)

d- I -- (*buy*)

H-Answer the questions أجب على الأسئلة :

   a- *Can Ali swim ?* : ----------------------- .

   b- *Can you jump off a wall ?* : ----------------------- .

   c- *Can Mona make a cake ?* : ----------------------- .

   d- *Can your father buy a car ?* : ----------------------- .

   e- *Can your mother drive a car ?* : ----------------------- .

I- Choose the right word. اختر الكلمة المناسبة

   a-   I (am - have - can) play football.

   b-   She can (feed – have – cake) cheese and bread .

   c-   He can (drive - drives) a car .

   d-   My father can (buy – sing – fly) a car.

   e-   My sister will (feed – drive - swim) her cat.

Lesson 60 الدرس الستون

a- Where do we get food from ?

A- Listen , read and <u>understand</u> : استمع واقرأ وافـهم

      1   2   3

Hello , I'm Ali . <u>Let me</u> <u>tell you</u> <u>something</u> .

        4

 Food is <u>good for you</u>. For you and for me .

         5

Food is good <u>for all people</u>. We need food . Why ?

        6   7

We need it <u>to live</u>. We live on food. <u>But</u> , we need

  8

<u>many kinds of</u> food .

                                  9   10

We need bread . We need <u>vegetables</u> *like*

tomatoes lettuce   l

cucumbers

         11   12

But where do we <u>get them</u> *from ? We get them from*

  13

<u>plants.</u>   ↓

(المقصود الخضراوات السابقة)

١- دعني / ٢- أخبـركم / ٣- شيئاً / ٤- صالح لكم / ٥- لـكل النـاس
٦- لكي نعيش / ٧- ولكن / ٨- أنواع كثيرة / ٩- الخضروات / ١٠- مـثل
١١- نحصل عليها / ١٢- مـن / ١٣ – النباتات /

a- Answer the questions   أجـب على الأسـئلة:

1- What do people need ? -- .
2- Why do people need food ? -------------------------------- .
3- Do people need many kinds of food ? --------------------
4- What vegetables do we need ? --------------------------------
5- Where do we get vegetables from ? ---------------------------

b- Tick (√) or (X) :

 1- Food is good for people.   (   )
2- Food   is not good for you.   (   )
3- Food   is good for some people.   (   )
4- People don't need food.   (   )
5- Bread is good for me.   (   )
6- Tomatoes are vegetables.   (   )
7- We get plants from vegetables   (   )

B- Fill in the spaces with these words :

for   /   need / live / on / kinds

   1- We ------------------ food.
2- We eat food to ------------ .
3- People live ---------- food.
4- We need many --------------- of food.
5- Food is good -------------- people.

***C-*Put these words into the correct order :**

1- is / for / good / you / Bread /

--- .

2- vegetables / People / need /

-- .

3- are / Cucumbers / kinds / vegetables / of /

--- .

b-Where do we get food from ?

 A-Listen , read and understand :

People need meat to live. But, where do we get it from? We get meat from animals like cows , goats , sheep and camels. We get meat from rabbits , chickens, ducks and geese . We get meat from fishes. Fishes live in the sea. We also get eggs from chickens. We also get milk and

butter from cows and goats. We make cheese from milk.

B- Answer the questions أجب على الأسئلة :

1- Do people need meat ? ------------------------------- .

2- What do we get from cows ? -------------------------------

3- Where do we get eggs from ? ------------------------------- .

4- What do we get from goats ? ----------------------------------

5- What do we make from milk ? ---------------------------

C- Put (√) or (X) :

1- We don't need meat .   (   )
2- We eat fish .   (   )
3- Fishes live in the sea.
4- We get milk and meat from cows.   (   )
5- We get eggs from goats.   (   )
6- We make milk from cheese.   (   )
7- We get meat from rabbits .   (   )
8- We eat meat from sheep and ducks. (   )

D-Fill in the spaces :

1- This is a ----------------- .

2- We ----------------- fish. It is good food.

3- ----------------- live in the sea .

4- We ----------------- meat ----------------- sheep.

5- We get milk ----------------- cows.

6- We get ----------------- and meat from ducks .

E-Choose the right word :

1- A fish (live –lives) in the sea.

2- Fishes (lives – live) in water.

3- Fish (is – are) good food.

4- This (is – are) a goat .

5- (This – These) are goats.

6- A sheep (is – are) under the tree.

7- I can see two (sheep- sheeps) .

8- We get meat from (goose – geese)

9- I want to feed this (geese – goose).

10- Sheep (is – are) good for us.

11- Geese (are- is) good for people.

F- Find the word أوجد الكلمة :

1- reduckes / 2- desheepio 3- segoatom

4- kcowes 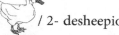 / 5- azcamelk 6- demchicken

7- vemilko / 8- gebutterem 9- tcheesed

G- Write a word under the picture أكتب كلمة تحت الصورة

----------------- ----------------- ----------------- -----------------

----------------------- ----------------- ----------------- -----------------

H- Fill in the spaces : أملأ الفراغات

1- I can ----------------------- a camel .

2- We get --------------- from chickens.

3- We get meat and milk from ---------------------- .

4- Lettuce and cucumbers are -------------------------- .

5- I can ---------------------- a car.

6- We -------------- meat with a knife.

7- We get milk from -------------------- and --------------- .

8- The weather is sunny. I need an ------------------------------ .

9- It is too hot. I have to ------------------------------- my A / C.

10- I have -------------------- and ---------------------- for breakfast.

الـدرس الثاني والستون   Lesson 62

c- Our food   غذاؤنا

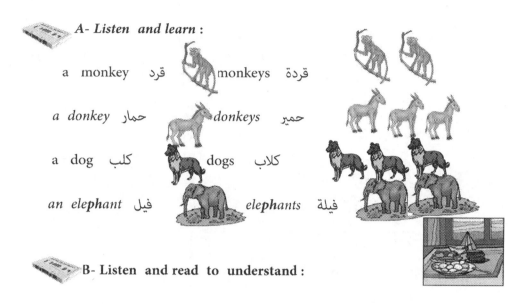

A- Listen and learn :

a monkey   قرد   monkeys   قردة

a donkey   حمار   *donkeys*   حمير

a dog   كلب   dogs   كلاب

an elephant   فيل   elephants   فيلة

B- Listen and read to understand :

Food is good for people. Meat is good food , but meat from dogs and cats is not good for people. Meat from donkeys is bad for us. We don't eat meat from elephants or horses.

We don't eat meat from monkeys or donkeys, but we eat meat from cows , sheep and chickens.

We don't eat meat from donkeys , horses or elephants , but we can ride them. We can ride a donkey , but we don't eat the meat from this animal.

a- ***Answer the questions*** أجـب عـلى الأسئـلة :

1- Is meat from cows good ? ---------------------------------------

2- Is meat from sheep good or bad ? ----------------------------

3- Is meat from dogs good ? --------------------------------------

4- Do we eat meat from monkeys ? -------------------------------

5- What animals can we ride ? ------------------------------------

b- Fill in the spaces :

1- We ------------ eat meat from donkeys.

2- We don't eat meat from monkeys or ---------------- .

3- We ---------------- meat from sheep.

4- We ---------------- donkeys and elephants.

5- We don't ---------------- sheep or goats.

C- Re-order these words :

1-   is / from / good / cows / Meat /

2-   from / get/ sheep/ We / meat/

3-   milk / get / We / cows / from.

4-   from / dogs / bad / is / Meat /

5-   can / donkeys / We / ride /

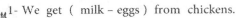

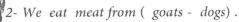

D- Choose the right words :

1- We get (milk – eggs) from chickens.

2- We eat meat from (goats - dogs) .

3- We don't eat meat from (sheep - horses).

4- Meat from cows is (bad- good).

5- We don't eat meat from (monkeys – ducks).

d- Our food .... Where do we get it from ?

A- Listen and read to understand :

Let me tell you more . We get some food from trees and plants. We get vegetables like tomatoes, lettuce and cucumbers.

We get fruit like apples , dates , oranges , bananas ,

melons and grapes .

Vegetables are good for you. Fruit is good too. Don't forget to eat fruit and vegetables every day.

Don't forget honey . It is good for you. Bees make this honey for us. I want you to eat dates , milk and honey. You'll benefit a lot.

Key words: كلمات رئيسية

more / المزيد   plants النباتات   fruit فاكهة

dates التمر   / grapes عنب / أيضاً

Don't forget   es النحل   honey العسل / لا تنسى

benefit يستفيد / كثيراً / every day كل يوم / melons البطيخ   *a lot*

B- *Answer the questions* أجب على الأسئلة :

1- What do we get from trees and plants ?

2- *What fruit do we get from trees ?*

3- What do bees make ?

4- What do you tell people to eat ?

C- Put (√) or (X) :

1- We get vegetables from cows.   (   )
2- *We get fruit from trees.*   (   )
3- We eat fruit and vegetables.   (   )
4- Grapes are a kind of fruit.   (   )
5- Honey is bad .   (   )
6- Dogs make honey.   (   )
7- I want you to eat dates and honey.   (   )
8- Melons are good food.   (   )

D- *Write a word under the picture* :

------------   ------------   ------------   -----------   -------------   --------

E- Classify these words : صنف هذه الكلمات

dog   melon   lettuce   apple   horse

tomatoes   grapes   mel   cucumber

Fruit	Animals	Vegetables
-------------------	-------------------	------------ ----
-------------------	-------------------	-------------------
-------------------	-------------------	-------------------

F- Write the missing letters أكتب الحروف المفقودة :

1- d ---- t---- s   2- el ---- ph---- nt

3- ---- rap---- ----   --- nk---- ----

5 d---nk--- ---   6- go ---- ts.

G- Re-order these words :

1- are / for / good / people/ Vegetables /

2- eat / every / honey / I / day /

3- for / honey / us / make / Bees /

4- is / people / for / Fruit / good /

5- like / and / I / grapes / dates /

H- Correct what's wrong : صحح الخطأ

rabt : ----------------   *danky* : ----------------

frut : ----------------   *_y* : ----------------

peaple : ----------------   *klimb* : ----------------

rite : ----------------   *_h* : ----------------

I- Oral Practice : تدريب شفوي

a : What do we get from bees ?
b : --------------------------.

a : Is it good or bad ?
b : --------------------------.

a- Can you ride an elephant ?
b- -------------------------- .

a- Can you write English ?
b- -------------------------- .

a- What do you like to eat ?
b- -------------------------- .

a- What do you like to drink ?
b- -------------------------- .

a- What is the weather like ?
b- -------------------------- .

الدرس الرابع والستون 64 Lesson

You are thirsty . What do you need ?

 A- Listen , read and understand:

I am Ali . You are **thirsty** . What do you need ?
<u>Of course</u> , you need water . But what kind of water ?
You <u>**look for**</u> fresh water . We drink <u>**fresh**</u> **water** .
We don't drink <u>**salt**</u> **water** . We can't drink salt water .
Where do we get fresh water from ?

*We get **fresh water** from **a river** .* نهر

*We get fresh water from **a lake**.* بحيرة
*We get fresh water from **rivers and lakes**.*

*We get fresh water from   **a well** .* بئر

*We get fresh water from   **a spring** .* نبع

We get fresh water from **wells and springs**.

We drink fresh water . We live on food and   water .

We can't live **without water** .

a river نهر / rivers أنهار , a lake بحيرة / lakes بحيرات

١٤٩

B- Listen and learn these words :

thirsty عطشان / fresh water مياه عذبة / salt water مياه مالحة

a river نهر / a well بئر / a spring نبع ماء /

without water بدون الماء

C- Answer these questions :

1- What do people drink ? --------------------------------------

2- Do people drink salt water ? ----------------------------------

3- You are hungry جوعان. What do you do ?

4- You are thirsty عطشان. What do you do ?

--.

5- Where do we get fresh water from ?

--.

D- Put (√) or (X) :

1- I'm hungry . I want salt water.　　(　)
2- I'm thirsty . I want fresh water.　　(　)
3- We drink salt water.　　(　)
4- We drink fresh water.　　(　)
5- We can live without water.　　(　)

E- Put these words into the spaces :

salt / without / fresh / rivers / thirsty / need

1- We are ---------------- . We need ----------------- water.

2- We can't live -------------------- water.

3- We --------------------food and water to live.

4- We get fresh water from wells and -------------------

5- We don't drink -------------------- water.

الدرس الخامس والستون Lesson 65

Water .....   What else do we need it for ?

Why do we use water ?   لماذا نستخدم الماء؟

 A- Listen and read to understand :

Look !   This boy is washing .

He needs water to wash.

We need water to wash. لكي نغتسل

Look ! This woman is washing dishes .

She needs water <u>to wash dishes</u> . لكي نغسل الصحون .

We need water **to wash clothes**. لكي نغسل الملابس

Look ! This woman is cooking food.

She is using water to cook meat . لكي نطبخ

We <u>use</u> water **to cook vegetables**. نستخدم

١٥١

Look ! This man is watering trees and flowers.
We use water **to water trees** and plants لكي نسقي
We water trees and plants to make them grow.

↓   ↓   ↓

نسقي   لكي نجعلها / تنمو

Look ! This is **a fireman**. هذا رجل مطافئ
He is **putting out** a fire. إنه يطفئ حريقاً
We use water **to put out** a fire.

↓

لكي نطفئ

B- Answer these questions :

1- Your hands are dirty وسخة . What do you need ?

2- Why do we use water ?

3- Your clothes are dirty . What do you need ? Why ?

I need -------------------- to -------------------- them.

4- You have some trees . What do you do ? Why ?

I -----------------------them to make them ----------------

5- You see a fire . What do you do ? How ? كيف ؟

I -- with water.

C- Fill in the spaces with these words :

washing / are / dirty / cook / use / need

1- The dish is ----------- . I will wash it with water.

2- The dishes ----------- dirty . I --------- some water
   to wash them.

3- I need some water to ------------------ the meat.

4- We can ------------------water to put out a fire .

5- This man is -------------------- his car with water.

D- Find the word أوجد الكلمة :

1- dofreshes   2- hesaltoy   3- voriveres

4- gowellyu   5- sespringer   6- rethirstyu

E- Write one sentence under each picture :   أكتب

جمـلة واحدة تحت كل صـورة .

-----------------------   -----------------------   -----------------------

-----------------------   -----------------------   -----------------------

-----------------------   -----------------------   -----------------------

-----------------------   -----------------------   -----------------------

The Sun

What is it ?

A- Listen , read and understand : استـمـع واقرأ وأفـهـم

The Sun is a star نجـم . *This star is bright* مضيء

This star shines. يشع

It gives off يشع *light* ضوء *and heat* حرارة .

We get light and heat from the Sun.

Light الضوء is good for people. We can see things .

We need light to see things.

The sunlight ضوء الشمس *is good for plants* النباتات *too* .

It helps them *grow.* إنها تساعدها على أن تنمو

(ينمو)

Heat الحرارة *is good for people.*

It keeps people warm. إنها تجلب للناس الدفء.

It helps plants grow.

But take care ! ولكن أحذر

Too much sunlight is bad for you.

Too much sunlight can get you ill.

Too much heat الحرارة الكثيرة جداً *is*

dangerous. خطيرة   *It can hurt you* , so keep

away from it.

Keep away from too much sunlight. ابتعد عن

Keep away from too much heat.

It can hurt you.→ إنها يمكن أن تؤذيك

B- Put (√) or (X) :

1- The Sun is a star . (   )

2- The Sun shines. (   )

3- We get food from the Sun. (   )

4- The sunlight is not good. (   )

5- We need light and heat . (   )

6- Too much sunlight is good for people. (   )

7- Too much sunlight is good for you. (   )

8- Plants need light and heat. (   )

9- We need light to see things . (   )

10- The sunlight kills plants. (   )

C- Fill in the spaces with these words:

bright / sunlight / dangerous / hurt / keep

1- Too much heat is ---------------------- .

2- This dog is mad, so -------------------- away from it .

3- This star is -------------------- .

4- Don't eat too much food ! This can --------------- you.

5- The -------------------- helps people see things.

D Learn and use this language   : تعلّم واستخدم هـذه اللغـة

too much food / too much heat / too much tea

* **too much** (كثير جداً) ← يأتي بعدها اسم مفرد لا يقبل الجمع

وفي هذه الحالة يستخدم للتعبير عن عدم الرضا من كثرة الشيء.

* I don't eat **too much meat**. It is bad.

* She doesn't want **too much money**.

* You drink **too much tea**. This is wrong.

*She talks **too much**. This is bad. إنها تتكلم كثيراً . إن هذا أمر سيئ

E- Use ' too much' :

1- Don't eat ----------------- . This is bad for you.

2- Don't talk --------------- . It is not nice.

3- Don't drink ------------------- tea. It is bad.

4- I don't eat --------------- food. It is wrong .

5- You want --------------- money. Why?!

6- We don't need ----------------- heat.

7- ---------------- sunlight is dangerous. Keep away from it.

F- Choose the right word   : اختر الكلمة المناسبة

1- The Sun is (kind – bright).

2- The Sun is a (plant – star).

3- The Sun gives off (light – right).

4- We need light and (hat – heat).

5- The sunlight helps plants (go – grow).

G. Put the words into the correct order :

1- is / much / bad / sunlight / Too /

2- from / heat / away / Keep /

3- keeps / warm / Heat / people.

4- get / We / from / Sun / light / the /

5- things / light / need / to see / We /

H- Write :

The sunlight is good for people .

We get light and heat from the Sun.

We need light to see things .

Light and heat are good for plants.

Too much sunlight is dangerous.

الدرس السابع والستون Lesson 67

How people travel

كيف يسافر الناس

A. Listen and learn :

People go to **other places.**   أماكن أخرى

People travel from one place to another.

الناس يسافرون من مكانٍ إلى أخر.

But how do they travel ?

Some people بعض الناس *travel* **by air.** جواً

They use planes.

This is comfortable مريحٌ *and fast* سريعٌ.

But it is expensive .   ولكنه غالٍ جداً

Some people travel **by sea.** بحراً

They use ships and boats.

براً   **Some** *travel* **by road.** البعض

They use trains , cars , buses and animals like مثل

camels , donkeys and horses.

This is slow بطئ ,*but cheap* رخيص.

Some travel **on foot.**   مشياً على الأقدام

This is not easy .   هذا ليس سهلاً

This is too hard .   هذا شاقٌ جداً

١٥٨

B- Tick (√) or (✗) :

1- *People travel from one place to another.* ( )
2- *Some people travel by plane.* ( )
3- *Some people travel by sea.* ( )
4- *Some people travel by car.* ( )
5- *Some people use dogs to travel.* ( )
6- *Some people use camels to travel.* ( )

*C- **Learn how to use this language** تعلّم كيف تستخدم هذه اللغة*

from one place to another من مكان إلى أخر

I went from one place to another.

from one house to another .

from one room to another .

from one car to another.

Fill in the spaces :

1- *We can travel from ----------- place to -----------*
2- *He went from one -------------- to ------------------*
3- *They took me from --------- room to --------------*
4- *I can take you from -------- city مدينة ----------------*
5- *He will take you --------- one park to ----------------*

*a. **Answer these questions:***

1- *How do you come to school ?* ------------------------

2- *How does Ali come to school ?* -----------------------

3- *How does Hamad go to the park ?* -----------------------

4- *How are they going to Dubai ?* ----------------------

5- *How are they travelling ?* -------------------------

D- Listen and repeat :

Ali: How do you come to school , Hamad ?

Hamad : On foot. I walk to school .

Ali: Why don't you go by bus ?

Hamad :   *Because my house is **close to** school .* قريبة من

Ali   :   But Mona comes by car.

Hamad : *That's right. Her house is too **far from** the school.*

بعيد عن ↓

Ali   :   How do you go to Oman ?

Hamad :   Of course , by plane .

Ali   :   By plane ? Why ? Why don't you go by car?

Hamad : *I **prefer** to go by plane . It's **comfortable** and fast.*

Ali   :   *That's right . But it's too **expensive**.*

Hamad : *The car is **cheap** , but it's too **hard** .*

Ali: You have money , Hamad . You don't care about

   *money . You **care about** comfort .*

إنك تهتم بالراحة

A- Read these sentences :

1- Look ! A woman **is washing** the dishes.

2- Look ! A man **is putting out** a fire.

3- The boys **are playing** football now.

4- I **am reading** a book now.

* انظر إلى الأفعال التي تحتها خط تجد ما يأتي :

١-إضافة -ing إلى الفعل الأصلي. / wash+ing , - / read +ing /

٢- استخدام فعل مساعد مثل : am / is / are حسب الاسم (الفاعل) الذي
يسبقه. ويجب مراعاة الانسجام بين الاسم والفعل المساعد كما هو مبين فيما يلي.

*   I **am reading** a book now.

*   Ali (هو He) **is reading** a book now.

*   Mona (هي She) **is cooking** now.

*   We نحن **are washing** the dishes now.

*   You أنتم-أنت **are washing** the car now .

*   They إنهم-إنهن **are washing** the car now .

٣- في وجود look ! أو now لابد من أن يكون الفعل في الشكل السابق.

* **Look !** A man is washing a car.

* They are playing football **now** .

* لاحظ كيف نضيف -ing و نراعي التغير في بعض الأفعال.

*go → going / do → doing / eat → eating /

ride → riding / drive → driving / write → writing

put → putting / run يركض→ running / swim يسبح →
swimming

B- Choose the right word :

1- Ali (am - is) tall . He is (play – playing) basketball.

2- I (is – am) hungry. I am (look - looking) for food.

3- You are (read – reading) a book now.

4- Look ! They are (run – running) .

5- Look ! A cat (is – am) climbing a wall.

* ادرس الجمل التالية و لاحظ الفرق :

1- *I* **play** *football* **every day.**

   I **am playing** football **now.**

الجملة الأولى تفيد بأن من عادتي أن ألعب كرة القدم كل يوم .

الجملة الثانية تفيد بأنني ألعب كرة القدم الآن.

2- *Ali plays football* **every day.**

   Look ! Ali **is playing** football.

3- *You* **always** *feed the horse.*

   You **are feeding** *the horse* **now.**

* ملاحظة: مع *always – every day* فإننا نستخدم الفعل الأصلي مثل *play- feed*

إلا أننا نضيف *s-* أو *es-* إلى الفعل الأصلي إذا جاء مع

(*he –Ali / she- Mona / it- car*)

* *I* always **drink** *fresh milk* .

* Ali **drinks** fresh milk every day.

* *I* **go** *to school every day* .

* *She* **goes** *to school every day.*

C -Choose the right verb :

1- I (eat - eating – eats) bread every day.
2- Ali always (come - comes – coming) to school .
3- Look ! Ali is (comes- come – coming).
4- The cat always (run – runs- running) here .
5- Look ! The cat is (runs – running – run) .
6- Hamad (like- likes) honey .
7- They (drinks – drink – drinking) fresh milk every day.
8- They are (have - having – haves) lunch now.
9- Ali (doing - do – does) his homework every day.
10- Ali is (does – doing – do) his homework now.

D- Write the correct verb - from اكتب الشكل الصحيح للفعل
1- *Ali always (play) --- ------------------ here.*
2- *Mona (drink) --------------------- milk every day.*
3- *My horse (jump) --------------------- every day.*
4- *This dog always (run) --------------------- after my cat.*
5- *A boy is (swim) --------------------- now.*
6- *A man is (put) --------------------- books on a table.*
7- *I want to (go) --------------------- home.*
8- *I always (feed) --------------------- my horse.*
9- *Ali will (feed) --------------------- the horse tomorrow.*
10- *We can (buy) --------------------- a small car.*

E- Re-order the words أعد ترتيب الكلمات :
1- is / the / Mona / dish / washing /

2- *am / my / feeding / horse / I /*

3- are / football / now / boys / playing / The /

4- feed / day / horse / every / I / my /

5- day / Mona / milk / every / drinks /

الدرس التاسع والستون Lesson 69

What are you doing ? ماذا تفعل؟

 A- Listen and understand :

Ali : What are you doing , Hamad ?

Mona: I'm reading a book.

Ali : What is mum doing ?

Mona: She's cooking .

Ali : What's she cooking ?

Mona: She's cooking meat and rice.

Ali : What are you doing , Mona ?

Mona: I'm helping mum in the kitchen.

Ali : Great !

B-Answer the questions :

1- What is Mona doing ? --

2- What is mum doing ? --

3- Where are Mona and her mother ?---------------------------

4- Is mum cooking meat ?--------------------------------------

5- Who is reading a book ? ------------------------------------

C- Read the questions and see how to answer them :

1- *What is* <u>Mona</u> *doing* ?
   ↓   ↓
        She is helping mum.

2- *Where is* <u>mum</u> *cooking* ?
        ↓
        She is cooking in the kitchen.

3- *Where are* <u>the boys</u> *going* ?
        ↓
        They are going to school.

4- *Who* <u>are you</u> *talking to* ?   لمـن تتحدث؟
        ↓
        I am talking to my father.

5- *What* <u>are you</u> *talking about* ?   عن ماذا تتحدثان؟
        ↓
        We are talking about the weather.

D- Answer the questions :

1- What is the cat doing ?

   -- .

2- Where are the girls going ?

   -- .

3- What are the dogs doing ?

   -- .

4- What are the men doing ?

   -- .

5- What are you doing ?

   -- .

E-Fill in the spaces to make questions :

* تذكّر أن شكل الفعل (play – playing) هو الذي يحدد استخدام الفعل المساعد على تكوين السؤال.

1- What ------------ the man doing ?

2- What ------------ you doing ?

3- Where are you -------------- ?

4- What does Huda ------------- ?

5- What --------- you drink every day ?

6- What does Hamad ------------- every day ?

7- Where --------- you go in the morning ?

8- When does ------------- watch TV ?

9- ------------- you always milk تحلب the cow ?

10- ------------- the boy always feed the cow ?

11- ------------- the boy feeding the cow now ?

F- Match a sentence to a picture :

1- The boys are playing football . ( )

2- My father is praying . ( )

3- A girl is drinking milk . ( )

4- My mother is cooking . ( )

5- A man is painting a door . ( )

الدرس السبعون Lesson 70

b- Grammar

* نحتاج لبناء الجملة إلى ثلاثة أشياء : اسم noun و فعل verb و صفة adjective
* الاسم مثل: Ali - Mona - book - car - cat – cats - tree- water
* وهناك ضمائر تحل محل الاسم مثل :
(I – me أنا) / (you أنت) / (he - him هو - وتحل محل اسم رجل)
(she - her هي – وتحل محل اسم أنثى) / (it - it هو – هي – إنه-إنها / وتحل
محل اسم مفرد غير عاقل مثل (car- book – tree – cup – meat
(we – us نحن) / (they – them هم – هن – إنهم – إنهن وتحل محل أي اسم
في الجمع مثل : cars - books - boys- sheep - geese – men – children

Pronouns الضمائر

* الضمائر إما أن تكون فاعلاً أو مفعولاً :

الفاعل		المفعول
I	→	me
He	→	him
She	→	her
It	→	it
You	→	you
We	→	us
They	→	them

How to make a sentence كيفية تكوين الجملة

a- Noun هناك نموذجان للجملة وهما :

(اسم يكون فاعلاً) → Noun فعل → Verb (اسم يكون مفعولاً به)

I	eat	meat .
Ali	eats	fish.
You	eat	apples.
The boys	play	football .
I	like	milk .
I	can't drink	it. (milk)
You	like	Mona.
I	don't like	her. (Mona)
I	will wash	the dishes.
Mona	will dry	them . (the dishes)
The man	is feeding	his horse.

b- Noun (اسم)→ Verb (فعل خاص بالصفات)→ Adjective (صفة)

I	am	tall. (طويل)
Ali (= He)	is	short. (قصير)
Mona (= She)	is	short .
The car (= It)	is	small. (صغيرة)
The dog	is	small.
The boys (= they)	are	small.

A- choose the right verb :

1- I can ------------- football .   (play – playing)

2- We ------------- food and water.   (need- needing)

3- Mona will ------------- the dish.   (wash – washes)

4- I can ------------- a horse.   (ride - riding)

5- A man is ------------- a car.   (drive – driving)

6- These apples ------------- green and red. (is- are)

7- I ------------hungry.جوعان   (is- am)

8- Ali ------------ short.   (is- are)

9- You ------------ thirsty.   (are – is)

B- Choose the right word:

1- I see Hamad at school . (He - She) comes by bus.

   I play football with (he – him) every day.

2- I (am - need) a car.

3- I (am - drink) fresh water.

4- I (am - eat) hungry,

5- Ali and Hamad (is - are) hungry.(He-They)need food.

6- This water is (tall – fresh – drink) .

7- This girl is (cook - cooking) meat.

8- These girls (is - are) tall.

9- Ali likes (I - me).

10- Ali (buy – buys) fresh milk.

C- Correct what's wrong صحح الخطأ :

1- I feeding my horse every day . ----------------

2- Ali is wash his hands now .   ----------------

3- I can riding a horse .   ----------------

4- I will doing my homework.   ----------------

5- We needing fresh water.   ----------------

6- We get fresh water from wills.   ----------------

7- We get milk from bees.   ----------------

8- The boy are going home.   ----------------

9- I have lunch in home .   ----------------

10- I use water to washing dishes.   ----------------

C- Grammar

* ملاحظات مفيدة :

١- سبق أن عرفنا بأنه يتم استخدام *don't* و *doesn't* في حالة النفي مع أفعال مثل:
drink , eat , go , mend , swim , play ,like , see , buy , climb .

1- I **drink** salt water .

I **don't drink** salt water.

2- You **don't drink** tea.

3- We **don't play** football at school.

4- They **don't see** Hamad at school.

5- Ali **doesn't like** tea.

6- Mona **doesn't eat** meat.

7- This cat **doesn't like** milk.

٢- يتم استخدام do و does في حالة السؤال مع الأفعال التي وردت في الملاحظة الأولى وأمثالها .

1- I drink milk .   (نعتبر هذه الجملة إجابة على سؤال)

↓

Do you drink milk ?   هل تشرب الحليب ؟   ← الجواب

Yes, I do. أو

No , I don't.

What do you drink ?   ماذا تشرب ؟   (الإجابة هي الجملة الأولى)

Where do you drink it ?   أين تشربه؟

When do you drink it ?   متى تشربه؟

2- He drinks milk at home.

↓

Does Ali drink milk ? ←الجواب (*Yes, he does.* أو *No, he doesn't.*)

What does Ali drink ? → الجواب *He drinks milk.*

Where does he drink it ? → الجواب *He drinks it at home.*

* نستخدم does و doesn't مع he (Ali) , she (Mona) , it(cat)
* اصنع أسئلة مماثلة متتبعاً الخطوات السابقة.

A- Use " don't " or " doesn't " :

1- The boys **go** to school every day.

2- This boy **goes** to school .

3- Fatma **likes** tea.

--.

4- You **mend** broken bikes.

--.

5- My father **help**s me with my homework .

--.

B- **Write questions** : أكتب الأسئلة

1- -- ?

    Yes , I do .

2- -- ?

    I have lunch at home.

3- -- ?

    They have meat and rice .

4- -- ?

    She gets up at five o'clock .

5- -- ?

    No , he doesn't.

C- Choose the right verb-form :

1- Where does he (lives – live) ?

2- What kind of water do we (drinks – drink) ?

3- Does Ali (need – needs) food ?

4- Where (do- does- is) she going ?

5- When (do – does – is) he come here ?

6- What is Mona (cook – cooking) ?

7- Where are you (go – going) ?

8- Where do you (go- going) ?

9- Who is (wash- washing) the car ?

10- Does Mona (feed – feeding) the horse ?

D- *Find the words* أوجد الكلمات :

1- defeeding

2- seridinged

3- sacookingmt

4- ferblacket

5- despringes

6- ceseaws

7- fordates

8- godonkey

9- frfatheres

E- Make sentences اصنع جملاً :

1- (*need* / *fresh*) : --------------------------------------

2- (*want* / *play*) : --------------------------------------

3- (*can* / *horse*) : --------------------------------------

4- (*feeding* / *horse*) : --------------------------------------

6- (*fresh*/ *drink* / *milk*) --------------------------------------

7- (*get* / *meat* / *cows*) --------------------------------------

8- (*bees* / *honey*) --------------------------------------

الدرس الثاني والسبعون Lesson 72

A- Listen and answer :

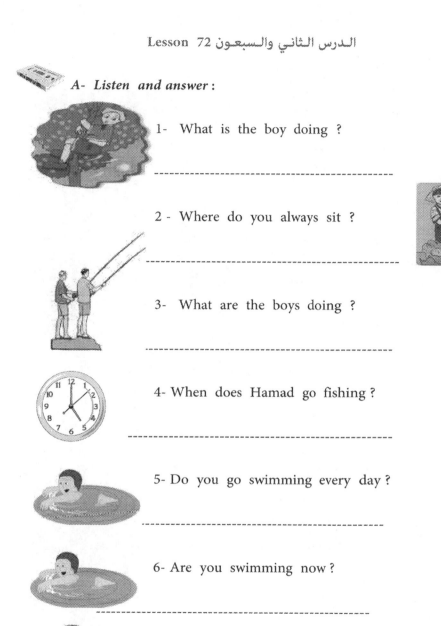

1- What is the boy doing ?

----

2 - Where do you always sit ?

3- What are the boys doing ?

4- When does Hamad go fishing ?

5- Do you go swimming every day ?

6- Are you swimming now ?

7- What are you doing ?

8- Is Hamad swimming now ?

١٧٣

B- Learn to tell the time : تعلّم طريقة إبلاغ الوقت :

 Listen :

Ali : *What's the time , Mona ?* ما الوقت يا منى؟

Mona: *It's five o'clock.*

Mona : Hamad , what's the time ?

Hamad: It's **twenty past three** . It's three twenty.

إنها الثالثة والثلث .

Hamad : *Mum , what's the time ,*<u>*please*</u> *?* من فضلك

Mum : *It's **half past five**.* إنها الخامسة والنصف

It's five thirty.

Mona : Dad , what's the time ,lease ?

Dad : *It's **ten to nine**.* إنها التاسعة إلا عشرة

It's eight fifty.

Mona : *Thank you , dad.* أشكرك يا والدي.

Hamad : Mona , what's the time ,please?

Mona : *It's **quarter to ten** .* إنها العاشرة إلا ربع

It's nine forty- five .

Hamad : Thank you , Mona.

C- **What is this ?**

*This is **a watch** .*
t's my watch.
can tell the time.

This is Mona's watch.
Mona can tell the time.

is is a clock .
e time is five past eleven.

This is an alarm clock .
This clock is good.
It wakes me every morning.   إنـها توقظني كل صباح.

D-   **Answer the questions :**

1- *Do you have a watch ?* ----------------------------------

2- *Can you tell the time ?* ----------------------------------

3- *Can Mona tell the time ?* ---------------------------------

4- What is the boy doing ?

5- *Why do you have a watch ?*

6- Why do you need an alarm clock ?

E-What's the time ?

 It's --- .

 It's --- .

F- Match a sentence to the correct time :

1- It's ten o'clock.

2- It's half past four .

3- It's five fifteen .

4- It's quarter to eleven.

G- Find the word   أوجـد الكـلمـة :

1-   vatchop   2-   noclockgh

3-   nytimeaf   4-   gohalfe

5-   fetellred   6-   mowakert

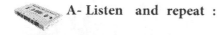 **A- Listen and repeat :**

Hallo. I'm Hamad . Today I want to tell you
الأسبوع / أيام
the days of the week. The week has seven days.
هنا أول أيام السبت
Saturday is the first day of the week **here** in Qatar.
الثلاثاء الاثنين الأحد
The other days are **Sunday** , **Monday** , **Tuesday** ,
الأربعاء الخميس الجمعة
Wednesday , **Thursday and Friday.**

We go to school **on Sunday.**
خمس مرات في الأسبوع
We go to school **five times a week.**

We don't go to school on Saturday or Friday.
في عطلة نهاية الأسبوع.
We don't go to school **at the week-end .**

B- Answer the questions :

1- How many days does the week have ?

2- What is the first day of the week ?

3- What is *the last day of the week* ? أخر أيام الأسبوع

١٧٧

4- Which days   أي الأيام   are week-ends ?

5- Do you go to school on Monday ?

6- Do you go to school on Friday ?

C- Fill in the spaces with these words : أملأ الفراغات بهذه الكلمات

days	on	first	times	at	last

1- The ----------------- day of the week is Saturday.

2- The week has seven ----------------- .

3- We always go to school ----------------- Sunday.

4- Friday is the ----------------- day of the week .

5- I don't go to school ----------------- the week-end.

6- I go to school five ----------------- a week.

D- Re-order these words :   أعد ترتيب هذه الكلمات

1- every / go / Sunday / school / I / to /

2- on / play / Friday / We / football /

3- don't / go / Monday / I / on / fishing /

4- last / is / day / Friday / the week / the / of /

5- at / I / my / the / see / week-end / friends الأصدقاء/

E- Put the days into the correct order رتب الأيام بالشكل الصحيح :

Sunday / Friday / Wednesday / Saturday /

Tuesday / Monday / Thursday /

1- ------------------------   2- ------------------------

3- ------------------------   4- ------------------------

5- ------------------------   6- ------------------------

7- ------------------------

F- Write a sentence under each picture
أكتب جملة تحت كل صورة

-----------------------   -----------------------   -----------------------

الدرس الرابع والسبعون Lesson 74
التحدث عن الماضي . Talking about the past
ماذا فعلت بالأمس ؟ ؟ What did you do yesterday

 A- Listen to Hamad :

أتحدث

 I am happy to **talk** *to you.*

فعلت

I **want** *to* **tell** *you what I* **did** *yesterday.*

أشياء كثيرة   كان

Yesterday **was** *a week-end . I* **did** <u>many things</u>.

قرب منزلي   في مطعم   تناولت

I **had** *breakfast* <u>at a take-away</u> <u>near my house</u>.

مع عائلتي   إلى الشاطئ

I **went** <u>to the beach</u> <u>with my family.</u>

I **played** *football at the park.*

زرت

I **visited** *some friends .*

I **watched** *TV .*

I **went** *shopping at The City Centre*
with my mother.

I **had** *a good time yesterday.*

أنا قضيت وقتاً ممتعاً يوم أمس.

B-Answer the questions :

1- Where did **Hamad have** breakfast ?
            ↓   ↓
          He   had breakfast at a take-away.

2- Where **was the take-away** ?
              ↓
          It was **near Hamad's house.**

3- Where did **Hamad go** with his family ?
            ↓   ↓
         He   went ---------------------- .

4- What did **he play** at the park ?
         He played --------------------.

5- Who did he visit ?

    --.

6- What did he watch ?

    --.

7- Where did he go shopping ?

--.

8- Who did he go shopping with ?

--.

C-Verb- forms : أشكال الفعل

** للفعل أربعة أشكال هي :

Present	Past	Past Participle	Present participle
play يلعب	*played* لعب	played	playing
wash يغسل	*washed* غسل	washed	washing
watch يشاهد	*watched* شاهد	watched	watching
visit يزور	*visited* زار	visited	*visiting*
clean ينظف	*cleaned* نظف	cleaned	cleaning
mend يصلّح	mended صلّحَ	mended	mending
climb يتسلق	*climbed* تسلق	climbed	climbing
go يذهب	went ذهبَ	gone	going
have يملك-يتناول	had	had	having
has = =	=	had	=
see يرى	saw رأى	seen	seeing
take يأخذ	*took* أخذ	taken	*taking*
get يحصل على	*got* حصل على	got	*getting*
feed يطعم	*fed* أطعم	fed	*feeding*
win يفوز	won فاز	won	winning
make يصنع	made صنع	made	making
do يعمل	did قام بـ – عمل	done	doing

* سبق أن استخدمنا الشكل الأول للفعل مع   every day / always ونلجأ إلى ذلك
عندما نتحدث عن عادة لدى الشخص أو حقيقة في الحاضر . أمثلة :

* I visit my friends every Friday .

* Ali always visits me .

* سبق أن استخدمنا الشكل   playing وما شابهه عندما نتحدث عن عمل نقوم به الآن
now . أمثلة:

* *Hamad is reading a book now.*

* <u>Look !</u> The boys are walking to school.

أما شكل الفعل في الماضي(أي الشكل الثاني) فإننا نستخدمه عندما نتحدث عن
شيء قمنا به في الماضي.

أمثلة :

* *I* **talked** *to Hamad* yesterday.   أنا تحدثت إلى حمد أمس.
* *They* **walked** *to school* last Monday.

إنهم مشوا إلى المدرسة الاثنين الماضي.

* *Mona* **drove** <u>to the beach</u> **last Friday**.

إن منى سارت بالسيارة إلى الشاطئ يوم الجمعة الماضية .

D- *Choose the right verb-form* :

1- I (go – going) to school by bus every day.

2- I (go - went – going) to the zoo yesterday.

3- She is (go – went – going) home now.

4- We will (go- went) fishing tomorrow.

5- I (see – saw) Mona at the park yesterday.

6- She (talk- talks – talked) to me last Sunday.

7- She always (talk – talks – talking) to me.

8- They are (talks – talking – talked) to Hamad.

9- I (get up – gets up) at five o'clock.

10- I (get up – got up) late yesterday.

E- *Find the word* :

1- foyesterdaymo   2- deFridayuo   3- dewenty

4- frnowe   5- deweeko   6- foedroveo

F- *Complete the sentence* أكمل الجملة :

1- I .... football every day.

2- I .... football yesterday.

3- I .... football now.

4- The boys .... to the beach last Sunday.

5- I .... my horse yesterday.

٨ - Listen and repeat :

Hamad : **Did** you **walk** to school <u>yesterday</u> ?

Mona : No , I didn't. I went by car.

Hamad : **Did** Salwa **talk** to you ?

Mona : No , she didn't.

Hamad : **Did** mum **help** you yesterday ?

Mona : Yes , she did .

Hamad : **Did** Jassim **talk** to you ?

Mona : Yes , he did.

Hamad : When **did** <u>Jassim</u> **talk** to you? متى تحدث جاسم إليك؟

↓   ↓   ↓

Mona : Last night . He talked to me last night.

انه تحدث لي الليلة الماضية.

Hamad : Where **did** you **go** with him ?

Mona : We went to the beach. إننا ذهبنا إلى الشاطئ.

Hamad : Why **did** you **go** there ? لماذا ذهبتما إلى هناك؟

↓   ↓   ↓

Mona : We went there <u>to relax</u> . لكي نستجم

Hamad : **Did** you **relax** ?

Mona : Yes , we did.

B- Answer the questions :

1- How did Mona go to school yesterday ?

2- Did she talk to Jassim ?

3- Did she talk to Salwa ?

4- Where did Jassim and Mona go ?

5- Why did Jassim and Mona go to the beach ?

C- Put (√) or (X) :

1- Mona walked to school yesterday.   (   )
2- Mum didn't help Mona.   (   )
3- Jassim didn't talk to Mona.   (   )
4- Salwa didn't talk to Mona .   (   )
5- Mona and Hamad went to the beach. (   )
6- Mona and Jassim relaxed at the beach. (   )

◄ ملاحظات : ١- إذا أردنا أن نسأل عن شيء حدث في الماضي , فإننا نستعين بـ
did مع مراعاة أن يكون الفعل في الشكل الأول. أمثلة :

* *Did you play football yesterday ?*
* *Did Mona talk to you last night ?*
* *Where did you go last Friday ?*
* *When did Jassim talk to you ?*

٢- في حالة النفي لفعل لم نفعله في الماضي , فإننا نستعين بـ didn't مع مراعاة أن يكون الفعل في الشكل الأول كما في الأمثلة التالية :

* I didn't go fishing yesterday.   إننا لم نذهب إلى الصيد أمس.

* Jassim didn't talk to me last Friday.

إن جاسماً لم يتحدث لي يوم الجمعة الماضية

* We didn't drink milk yesterday.

٣- نستخدم أدوات الاستفهام التالية :

what - ماذا – للسؤال عن شيء .

where- أين – للسؤال عن مكان .

when- متى- للسؤال عن الزمن .

who- من – للسؤال عن شخص أو أشخاص.

Why- لماذا – للسؤال عن سبب أو هدف .

How – كيف- للسؤال عن الحال أو الوسيلة .

D- Choose the right word :

1- (What - Who) do you drink ?

2- (Where- Who) did you go yesterday ?

3- (When – Who) did you talk to yesterday ?

4- (Where – What) are you doing now ?

5- (How –Who) do you come to school ?

6- (What – When) did you go ?

7- (How- What) do you need ?

8- (How- Why) do you need food ?

9- (Where – What) is my book ?

10- (Who- How) is washing the car ?

الـدرس السادس والسبعون   Lesson 76

A- Choose the right verb- form : اخـتر الشكل الصحيح للفعل

1- Did Jassim (go – goes – went) there yesterday ?

2- Where   did Jassim (went – go) last Friday ?

3-Where   did you (play – played) yesterday ?

4- Why did you (came - come) late yesterday ?

5- How (do- does- did) you come yesterday ?

6-(Do- Does – Did) Jassim help you yesterday ?

7- (Do – Does – Is) Ali help you ?

8- (Do – Does – Are) you help Jassim ?

9-What(do –did) you have yesterday morning ?

10-Where(do-does- did) Hamad go last night ?

B- Re-order these words : أعـد تـرتيـب هـذه الكلمات
1- see / Mona / dog / the / Did

--- ?
2- did / Ali / go / yesterday / Where /

--- ?

3- you / What / have / lunch / did / for ?
--- ?
4- Ali / you/ Does / to / day / every / talk /
--- ?

١٨٧

C-Fill in the spaces with words from this list :

أملأ الـفراغ بـكلمات مـن هـذه القائمة :

visited / drink / went / talked / go / every / last

1- I --------------------- to Hamad last night.

2- She talks to me -------------------- Friday.

3- Jassim -------------------- his friends yesterday.

4- My friends -------------------- to the beach yesterday.

5- Mona didn't -------------------- to the beach yesterday .

6- Did you -------------------- milk yesterday ?

D-Answer these questions :

1- Did you go to school yesterday ? -------------------------------

2- Did Jassim walk to school Yesterday ? ------------------------

3- Did Mona come to school last Friday ? -----------------------

4- Where did you go last night ? -------------------------------

5- Do you go to school on Friday ? -------------------------------

6- Does Mona like milk ? -------------------------------------

7- Is Mona coming to the party الحفلة ? ----------------------------

8- Can you come to my party ? -------------------------------

9- What will you buy tomorrow ? -------------------------------

10- Where is Jassim sitting ? -------------------------------

E-Make sentences :

1- (eat) : --

2- (drank) : --

3- (jumped off): --

4- (visited) : --

5- (feed) : --

6- (fed) : --

7- (feeding) : --

8- (do) : --

9- (ride) : --

10- (rode) : --

11- (talking) : --

12- (walked) : --

* نستخدم الشكل الثالث للفعل للحديث عن شيء حدث في الماضي ولكن لا تزال له
أثار في الحاضر . في حالة استخدام الشكل الثالث لا بد من استخدام :

have   أو   has

*   Examples أمثلة :

1-   I   *have washed* my car .   لقد غسلت سيارتي .

(التعليق : غسل السيارة تم , وها هي السيارة نظيفة)

2-   You *have broken* the window.   لقد كسرت أنت النافذة .
3-   Ali and Nasser *have won* the cup.   لقد فاز علي وناصر بالكأس.
4-   Ali *has talked* to his father .   لقد تحـدث علي إلى والده.
5-   Mona *has made* a cake .   لقد صنعت منى كيكاً .
6-   It *has rained* a lot.   لقد أمطرت الدنيا كثيراً.

have →   تستخدم مع   I , you أنت - أنتم ,   we نحن , they هم
has →   Ali (he) , Mona (she) , car , book cat (it)

I have won a prize .   (√)   لقد فزت بـجائزة.
Ali have won a prize.   (✗)
The cat has eaten my fish. (√)   لقد أكلت القطة سمكتي .

* I have not got the money.   لم أستلم النقود .
* She has not made a cake .   إنها لم تصنع كيكاً .
* A :   Have you cleaned the car ?   هـل نظفت السيارة ؟
  B : (Yes , I have .) أو   No , I haven't.
* A : Has Ali fed the cat ?

B : Yes , he has . أو (No , he hasn't.)

* A : What have you done ?   ماذا فعلت ؟
  B : I have washed my car.
       I have talked to my father.
       I have fed my horse.
       I have eaten my apple.

* A : What has Mona done ?
  B : She has cleaned her teeth.
       She has helped her mother.
       She has cooked the meat.
       She has won a prize.

* Choose the correct verb-form : اختر الشكل الصحيح للفعل

1- I have (wash – washed – washing) my car.
2- Hamad has (feeding – feed – fed) his horse.
3- We have (win – won) the race.
4- My father has (bought- buying – buy) a new car.
5- My friends have (write – wrote – written) the words.

Answer these questions :   أجب على هذه الأسئلة

1- Have you got a new book ?   ---
2- Has Ali eaten his apple ?   ---
3- Where has Mona gone ?   ---
4- What have you seen ?   ---
5- What have you done ?   --

Correct the mistakes   صحح الأخطاء :
1- I have kill a mouse.   ---------------------
2- Ali has feeding his camel.   ---------------------
3- We have playing a game.   ---------------------
4- My mother have cooked the meat.   ----------------------
5- Ali have cut a tree.   ----------------------

الدرس السابع والسبعون Lesson 77

التحدث عن الماضي Talking about the past

Where were you ... ؟ أين كنت؟

وماذا كنت تفعل؟ ؟ What were you doing

 A_-Listen and understand :

Hamad : *Where were you at five o'clock* ?

Mona : *I was in the park.*

Hamad : *What were you doing* ?

Mona : *I was walking with my friends.*

Hamad : *Did you enjoy that* ? هل استمتعت بذلك ؟

Mona : *Yes , I did .*

Hamad : *Where are you going* tomorrow ?

Mona : *We are going to the zoo .*

Hamad : Can I come ?
Mona : *You're welcome , Hamad.*
         What will you do there ?
Hamad : Of course , I'll see some animals.
I'll ride the elephant , my <u>favourite</u> animal. المفضل

B- Put (√) or (X) :

1- Hamad was in the park .   (   )

2- Mona was walking with Hamad.   (   )

3- Hamad is talking to Mona.   (   )

4- Mona enjoyed walking in the park . (   )

5- Mona is going to the park tomorrow. (   )

6- Hamad wants to go to the zoo.   (   )

C- Answer the questions :

1- Where was Mona ?

2- What was she doing ?

3- Where is Mona going tomorrow ?

4- What does Hamad want to do ?

5- What will he do there ماذا سيفعل هناك؟

6- What is Hamad's favourite animal ?

ملاحظة :

* نستخدم شكل الفعل مثل reading - feeding – playing مع was للمفرد
و were للجمع للحديث عن فعل كان مستمراً في وقت ما في الماضي . أمثلة :

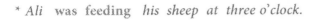

* I was reading *a book* at five o'clock.

* Ali was feeding *his sheep at three o'clock.*

* The boys were playing *football at two o'clock* .

* Ali **is reading** *a book* **now**.	(√)
* Ali **was mending** *his chair*.	(√)
* I was *mend my chair* .	(X)
* I **mend** my chair.	(√)
* I **mended** my table **yesterday**.	(√)
* I was mended my chair .	(X)
* I **will mend** my bike tomorrow .	(√)
* I can mend it .	(√)

D-Answer the questions :

1- What is Ali doing now ?

2- What was Ali doing at three o'clock ?

3- Where were the boys playing ?

١٩٤

4- Where is the boy sitting now?

5- What are you doing now?

6- Where were you going at three o'clock?

E-Correct the verb : صحح الفعل

1- Mona is (wash) ------------------------ the dish now.

2- I was (shop) ------------------------ at three o'clock.

3- We were (watch) ------------------------ a game.

4- I am (read) ------------------------ a book now.

5- They are (talk) ------------------------ to Ali.

6- They were (walk) ------------------------ to the farm.

7- I can (write) ------------------------ my name.

8- Mona always (help) ------------------------ me.

9- I (drink) ------------------------ fresh milk every day.

10- I didn't (drink) ------------------------ tea yesterday.

11- I (drink) ------------------------ milk yesterday.

12- She doesn't (walk) ------------------------ to school.

13- We will (talk) ------------------------ to the nurse.

14- They are (put) ------------------------ out a fire.

15- She was (cook) -------------------- meat at three o'clock.

16- I am (write) -------------------- now.

17- I (write) -------------------- something yesterday.

18- I have (write) -------------------- something. I am happy.

19- Mona has (get) -------------------- a new camera. She is happy.

20- We have (win) -------------------- the game. We are happy.

المحتويات The Index

Page	Content

Author's Biography   سيرة المؤلف

* *Born in Palestine 1n 1946.*   وُلدَ في فلسطين عام ١٩٤٦.

* Obtained his B.A. in English language & Literature
   from Cairo University in 1967 with grade " Good"

* حصل على درجة الليسانس في اللغة الإنجليزية و آدابها
من جامعة القاهرة بتقدير " جيد " عام ١٩٦٧ .

* Has been teaching English with Qatar's Ministry of
   Education since 1967.

* يقوم بتدريس اللغة الإنجليزية بوزارة التربية
والتعليم منذ العام ١٩٦٧ .

* Sent to Britain in 1967 on an in- service training course .

* أُرسل إلى بريطانيا في دورة تدريبية تتعلق بتدريس الإنجليزية
كلغة ثانية .

* Obtained his Education Diploma in English language
   teaching as a second language from Qatar University in
   1977 .

* حصل على دبلوم التربية في تدريس الإنجليزية
كلغة ثانية من جامعة قطر عام ١٩٧٧ .

* Has published four books.   نشر أربعة كتب

\# The Sound Approach to English Grammar.
   الطريقة المثلى لقواعد اللغة الإنجليزية
\# English for Beginners.   الإنجليزية للمبتدئين
\# Art of Writing.   فن الكتابة
\# A Simplified English – Arabic Glossary of Words in
Common Use

القاموس المبسط لكلمات متداولة

Printed in the United States
By Bookmasters